Event Marketing

The Wiley Event Management Series

SERIES EDITOR: DR. JOE GOLDBLATT, CSEP

Special Events: Twenty-first Century Global Event Management, Third Edition
by Dr. Joe Goldblatt, CSEP

Dictionary of Event Management, Second Edition
by Dr. Joe Goldblatt, CSEP, and Kathleen S. Nelson, CSEP

Corporate Event Project Management
by William O'Toole and Phyllis Mikolaitis, CSEP

*Event Marketing: How to Successfully Promote Events,
Festivals, Conventions, and Expositions*
by Leonard H. Hoyle, CAE, CMP

Event Risk Management and Safety
by Peter E. Tarlow, Ph.D.

Event Sponsorship
by Bruce E. Skinner and Vladimir Rukavina

The Complete Guide to Destination Management
by Pat Schauman, CMP, CSEP

Event Marketing

HOW TO SUCCESSFULLY PROMOTE EVENTS, FESTIVALS, CONVENTIONS, AND EXPOSITIONS

Leonard H. Hoyle, CAE, CMP

JOHN WILEY & SONS, INC.

Copyright © 2002 by John Wiley & Sons, Inc., New York. All rights reserved.

Published simultaneously in Canada.

Library of Congress Cataloging-in-Publication Data:

Hoyle, Leonard H.
    Event marketing : how to successfully promote events, festivals, conventions, and expositions / Leonard H. Hoyle.
      p. cm. — (The Wiley event management series)
    Includes bibliographical references and index.
    ISBN 0-471-40179-X (cloth : alk. paper)
    1. Special events—Marketing. I. Title. II. Series.

GT3405.H69 2002
658.4′56—dc21

          2001046819

Printed in the United States of America.

10 9 8 7 6 5 4 3 2 1

Dedication

This book is dedicated to my wife Judy, whose infinite patience and understanding permitted me the time and sanctity to prepare this volume. Come to think of it, it has been her patience and understanding that has allowed me to be involved in the events industry for 35 years. I can never repay her for her love, support, and constant encouragement. But I can dedicate this book to her, and gratefully I do.

Contents

Foreword

According to the management guru Peter Ferdinand Drucker, "Business has only two basic functions—marketing and innovation." Dr. Drucker understands that every business enterprise, whether not-for-profit or for-profit, must carefully research, design, plan, coordinate, and evaluate its marketing strategy to consistently achieve the goals of the enterprise.

Buck Hoyle also understands and in this pioneering book helps you to grasp and use the proven, successful principles of event marketing. Hoyle is the most qualified author to write this volume because he understands not only the theoretical underpinnings of this newly emerging discipline but also the practical requirements for promoting and selling events.

With over thirty years' professional experience in the event marketing field, Buck Hoyle has helped market meetings, conventions, conferences, expositions, and special events both large and small. He has served as chairman of the Convention Liaison Council (CLC), is a leader in the American Society of Association Executives (ASAE), and is a much sought after speaker for national associations in the event management industry, such as the Religious Conference Management Association.

Therefore, Mr. Hoyle is the leading expert in the field of event marketing, and this volume reflects his three decades of experience along with the best practices of dozens of other successful event management organizations.

The book includes many practical models that together form a system for event marketing that will ensure the future success of your events and make your recurring events even more profitable. Using the latest information regarding cyber event marketing (event e-commerce), he shows you how to easily and effectively use the latest technologies to reach your event's target market.

If your not-for-profit or for-profit enterprise occasionally or regularly brings people together for mutual benefit, this book provides the tools you will need to rapidly increase your success. As a result of this important new addition to the event management literature, Dr. Drucker's classic definition may now be expanded to combine marketing and innovation into one priceless opportunity. *Event Marketing* ensures that you can become the leading *marketing innovator* for your enterprise. As a result, you will soon redefine your own success in the event industry by using this valuable and important new tool.

Dr. Joe Goldblatt, CSEP
Series Editor, The Wiley Event Management Series
Dean & Professor, Johnson & Wales University

Preface

The Magic of Commitment

Without *commitment* there is hesitancy, the chance to draw back, always ineffectiveness.

But in all acts of initiative and creation, there is one elementary truth, the absence of which kills countless ideas and splendid plans. And that is that the moment one definitely *commits* oneself, then *providence moves too*, raising in one's favor all manner of unforeseen incidents, and meetings, and material assistance, which no man could have dreamed would have come his way.

I have a deep respect for one of Goethe's couplets:

Whatever you can do, or dream you can, begin it.
Boldness has genius, power and magic in it!
—W. H. Murray (1840–1904)

Early in my career in association and convention management, an older, wiser colleague shared this philosophy of commitment with me in the quiet sanctity of my office late one evening. He quoted it to me out of hand and from memory. That was 33 years ago. I never forgot it.

When he finished speaking, I was so taken with and compelled by this wisdom, I asked my mentor to repeat it. As he did, I frantically scribbled it on a lined legal pad. I found myself not only trying to practice Mr. Murray's creative concepts in my work, but also found myself sharing his words about commitment and synergistic support with others in my writings, speeches, classroom lectures, and even casual conversations.

I had that same sheet of lined paper with the fading and blotched ink on my desk for years. In those moments of doubt in

my work or my life, I would revisit it for inspiration. My super-
stitions forced me to keep the original wrinkled draft under my pa-
perweight. I did copy it in the computer and in my calendar—just
in case—but the old faithful inscription was there for me, on my
desk, close at hand. It was folded, spindled, and mutilated from
years of handling, but nonetheless was a foundation for my pur-
suits and my beliefs. For more than 30 years, I have treasured that
late-evening conversation with my old friend, and what I learned
from it. I still do.

Why? In event management, and particularly within the marketing discipline, all of the ingredients of success or failure are in
those few sentences. Commitment to your goal is essential to full
achievement. It generates excitement, creativity, and infectious enthusiasm. It draws others to your objectives, bringing to you new
resources, people, and support that synergistically amplify your
efforts. And this help will come from places you may not always
anticipate. But, as an event manager and marketer, it must start
with you.

To ensure success over the long term, reject the notion that
things should always be done as they have been done before. You
must *dream* what that event can be. Design it according to your
vision. Describe your concepts to your friends and colleagues,
supporters, and sponsors. Determine their levels of interest. And
with those for whom you detect the highest levels of interest and
support, learn to "ask for the order." This text will help you
do that.

Be bold! Don't be afraid to dream and put those dreams into
action. And feel the "genius, power, and magic" that your events
will produce for others.

Build It, and They Will Come

In 1989, Universal City Studios released the motion picture *Field
of Dreams.* Starring Kevin Costner, Amy Madigan, James Earl Jones,
Burt Lancaster, and Ray Liotta, the movie was a glowing tribute to
all who dare to dream. For me, it revalidated W. H. Murray's philosophy of commitment and creativity, and I was struck by the
film's mantra: ***"If you build it, they will come."***

The foundation of the film is a baseball diamond carved out of a cornfield on a Dyersville, Iowa, farm some 20 miles from Dubuque. The ball field lures a myriad of people in the motion picture, all seeking to fulfill individual dreams in a most unlikely, hard-to-reach place. They do realize their dreams, in a hauntingly mystical and magical way.

What does this have to do with marketing?

First, the concept that "this is the place where dreams come true" has captured the imagination of literally millions of people. So much so that now, *more than 12 years later,* the actual movie site of the baseball field is still maintained by the original farmers in the middle of a cornfield, just as it was during the shooting of the film. The only alterations to this pristine site are the parking lots for the vans and buses that bring tourists, even today, from April to November and the concession stands that serve and sell to them.

Second, the people who to this day still find their way by the busload and carload to this "middle of nowhere" cornfield in central Iowa are active, not passive, participants. They are encouraged to take to the field, grab a ball and bat, and have a game of catch. Just like when you were a kid! Relive a dream of glory on the ball field. Meet some new people. Have some fun!

They are encouraged to wander into the cornfield, pick an ear of corn, dig up a little of the soil, and take it home to remember the experience. *Make the experience memorable.* That may be the most basic law of effective event management and marketing.

Third, the concept itself is *original.* It is something *different.* In the increasingly crowded field of special events and the growing challenges of marketing those events against growing competition, originality is critical to success. It is the unique experience that will become memorable for those who participate in it.

I had an old friend who wrote this "first commandment" to market his destination management and event production company in Mexico:

Thou Shalt Not Expect to Find Things as Thou Hast Them at Home, For Thou Hast Left Home to Find Them Different.

Owing to arrangements made by my wife who responded to the innovative marketing of, and my fascination with, the lure of that cornfield in Iowa, I was able to visit personally the "Field of

Dreams" on a bitter-cold October day. I was drawn there by the original creative concept, the chance to do something that would be memorable to me forever, and the idea of being an active participant with others. Despite fighting the frigid winds, we did have a game of catch with people we knew and others we had never met before.

It was so great! It filled my soul with the essence of human interaction, the capturing of common interests in even the most unlikely of places, among people who were previously strangers. It created personal bonds that have lasted for years. And that is the essence of the event industry.

I still have the ear of corn mounted on my office wall to prove I was there. I'll probably never get to go back. But in a way, I'll never leave.

What does this have to do with event marketing?

As examples: Today, the "Field of Dreams" not only attracts tourists by the busload, but also is the site for all-star baseball games, weddings, receptions, parties and various celebrations, reunions, and other special events. Their integrated marketing technique is employed throughout Iowa, including concentrated cooperative marketing with the Dubuque Convention and Visitors Bureau. And all of this happens in this unique venue, flanked only by a farmhouse, a corn silo, and a barn or two.

But I can give you a more personal example of the spirit of this special place. A few years after my visit to that cornfield in Iowa, I was involved in creating a totally new educational conference and exposition for a trade association I was managing. This effort would be a "leap of faith" that would likely decide the future of the organization, for good or for bad.

The new event would face severe competition from established associations running profitable, high-visibility conventions and expositions. The enterprise would require us to create an identity and name-brand recognition for our fledgling conference. It would necessitate the identification of new market segments and target-marketing strategies. No success was guaranteed. Failure was a definite possibility. Still, we pursued our market analyses and financial projections.

If anything, our industry colleagues and competitors were chuckling at our folly. We were about to commit more than $250,000 (all of our financial reserves) to the creation and marketing of a totally new event concept. And we were about to do that in the face of daunting and often unfriendly competition.

During my nights, sleep was elusive. I was doing much tossing and turning. Should we risk this? If it goes wrong, will I be held to blame? This was a defining moment for my association and for my career. And the answer came to me, believe it or not, one night in a fitful dream: *"If you build it, they will come."* The dream became crystal clear.

We could build the better mousetrap, the cutting-edge concept. We could design a more creative event that captures the imagination of our industry. We could take advantage of the chance to provide a memorable experience for attendees. We could design innovative ways for people to participate actively, rather than passively. We could make it a profitable experience for all, in terms of both money and sociological/career-development motivations. All of the lessons were there. And if we do it right, we could put our association on the map in terms of legitimacy and in the black in terms of finances.

The strategy for the launching of this event, Affordable Meetings Conference and Exposition, sponsored by the Hospitality Sales and Marketing Association International, required integrative marketing techniques, product design, and market research and segmentation.

This annual event has become an incredible success story—and all because of the event marketing and management principles of producing events that are *original, creative, participative, and memorable.*

"I'd Love to Throw Parties for a Living"

Nikolaj Petrovic loves to tell this story. Now the president and CEO of the International Association for Document and Information Management Solutions, Nik's background is event management and marketing for association and corporate conferences as well as reunions, expositions, fundraisers, and other special events.

He was at a reception, talking casually with several new acquaintances. They were discussing their respective professions, and one guest said that he was a lawyer. Another said that he owned several franchises. Still another was the vice president of a bank. When asked what he did, Nik answered, "I'm a convention planner." After a pause, one of his new friends said, "Boy! I'd love to throw parties for a living!" He never forgot that exchange.

He also regrets he never had a chance to rebut the implications of that "throwing parties" comment, because he knew the demands and disciplines of his work, and they didn't. He knew that every day he had to have a working knowledge of:

- Group dynamics
- Marketing, promotion, and publicity
- Financial management and accounting
- Politics and leadership management
- Food and beverage management
- Law and liabilities
- Site inspection and selection
- Transportation
- Facilities management
- Housing and reservations
- Registration procedures
- Contracts and insurance
- Program participants' and speakers' liaison
- Logistics, function rooms, and meeting space
- Shipping and drayage
- Audiovisuals, teleconferencing, and electronic communications
- "Show flows" and scheduling
- Master accounts and gratuities
- Staging and decorations
- Exhibit management and marketing
- Program planning
- Evaluation and analysis techniques

And that's just a *partial* list of the body of knowledge required of the professional event manager.

Whether you are involved in marketing a major convention/exposition for 20,000 people or planning a wedding reception for 200, many, if not all, of these disciplines will be your responsibility. In other words, there is much more to it than "throwing parties for a living." No wonder my friend Nik was insulted—and speechless—as a result of this comment.

Marketing: The Integrative Management Tool

There is an old adage that "Nothing happens until somebody sells something"—an observation offered by Red Motley, the original editor of *Parade* magazine, the Sunday supplement to the *Washington Post.* Nowhere is this truer than in the conference and event industry. The marketing process must begin at the outset of the planning process, during the setting of the goals and objectives of the event itself. Marketing must both *reflect* and *drive* those objectives. It must also integrate the objectives into one goal and enlist people into action toward the fulfillment of that goal.

For example, an educational conference essentially has one goal: to educate participants. The marketing approach should emphasize the unique educational programs that this event will offer the attendee. Many vague promotions begin with "You Are Invited to Attend. . ." or something limpid such as "Join Us for the 20th Annual Conference." These are far less compelling pitches than those that proclaim: "Learn How to Increase Your Profits" or "Ensure That Your Business Can Survive in the New Millennium."

A conference might be designed to focus on a number of objectives such as, for example, education, entertainment, and changing the future governance of the organization. If this is our hypothetical event, marketing should drive all of those objectives. As an example, print promotion should proclaim that when you attend this event, you will learn "Techniques for Success," revel in "The Greatest Celebration of the Decade," and discover how to "Position Our Association to Succeed in the New Millennium."

The essential point is that the marketing must begin when the planning process is launched. Only then can it serve as the greatest integral asset to drive attendance, profits, and repeat business at the next event.

EFFECTIVE MARKETING TAKES INTERNAL OBJECTIVES AND TURNS THEM INTO EXTERNAL RESULTS

Marketing should integrate all of the management decisions so that they focus on the goals and objectives of the event as well as those of the sponsoring organization itself. This integration may take many forms. It may be a subtle campaign to preconvince corporate shareholders or association leaders of the importance of their attendance and their personal vote on an issue. It may be employed to conduct research to assist in the event's site selection process. Marketing can play a vital role in the "search and discover" effort to identify new markets in which to promote an event. And, of course, it should include the other classic elements of marketing, such as advertising, telemarketing, and promotional campaigns, to bring all of the event goals to life.

In other words, the enlightened event professional will incorporate marketing at the outset of the planning process so that all goals, objectives, and strategies will be considered and amplified with marketing implications in mind. As you read this text, you will see how integrated marketing forms the glue that binds together the mission, functional implementation, final evaluation, and planning for future events. And you will learn the elements of an integrated marketing campaign.

The Multifunctional Discipline of Marketing

Few of us enjoy the opportunity to do only one thing in our jobs. As you pursue a career in event marketing, you will probably find yourself balancing that responsibility with many others that may be totally unrelated.

In his book *Special Events,* Dr. Joe Goldblatt offers this personal observation to students in his event management program at George Washington University in Washington, DC:

> *Many of the students who apply for admission to the Event Management program tell me that although managing events was but one of their job responsibilities it was the one they most enjoyed. Therefore, they are seeking further training in this profession to improve their chances for long-term success doing something they truly enjoy. In learning these highly portable skill sets they are simultaneously increasing their opportunities for long-term career success in many other professions as well.*

In this text, we will explore the many functions embodied in the marketing discipline. Among them are:

- Print media
- Electronic media
- Human dynamics
- Group dynamics
- Internal public relations
- External public relations
- Press relations
- Promotions
- Advertising
- Sales and merchandising
- Sponsorships
- Special celebrations
- And much more

You will find that the many other duties you have in your work will lead you to resources that can be of significant value to you in your event management and marketing responsibilities. That newspaper contact you have made in your government relations activities may help in placing a news release for an event you are charged with planning. The research firm that has been working to help your organization build membership may be a resource for building your promotional mailing list. The speaker that you heard at the annual meeting of a related association may be your next keynoter, providing you with a cornerstone for not only the event you must plan, but also the marketing materials you need to sell it.

It is no accident that the most successful people are also the busiest people. Remember the old saying: "The harder I work, the luckier I get." Your resources for event marketing are all around you. Be alert to the people, places, and properties that may make your next event one that is not only remarkable, but also memorable.

A "People" Business

So as we move through this study of marketing events and meetings, remember one thing: As you adopt this defining activity as your chosen profession, you are in the business of brain surgery.

Not as a medical doctor, but rather as a modifier of minds. Your events will make people happy through celebrations; make them smarter through education; make them collaborate through interaction; make them conciliate through arbitration; make them profit through motivation. The results of your efforts are limited only by your imagination and your drive.

It's a *people* business. If you are doing your job right, you are modifying minds and fulfilling dreams. And I know of no other sense of satisfaction, no other exhilaration that can match that of the event marketer who markets and manages well. And then when the event is over, he or she has to answer that age-old question: "How're you gonna top this next year?" Now, *that's* a great challenge! And *this* is a great career!

In Appreciation Of

Dr. Joe Goldblatt, CSEP, who, at his relatively tender age, has already become known worldwide as a patriarch of modern event management and marketing practices. Grabbing the sword and leading the charge toward completion of this book, he guided and encouraged me to stay the course and take the hill. I am forever in his debt.

JoAnna Turtletaub, whose timeless patience and cheerful support as our publisher's senior editor was such a significant asset during the writing, assimilation, and completion of the project.

Erin M. Turner is contributing author to Chapter 3, a testament to her experience and expertise in electronic event marketing strategies that unravel the mysteries of this revolutionary communications phenomenon.

Bill Knight is contributing author to Chapter 4. His understanding that little is possible without adequate event funding and exemplary budget practices attests to the success of his event management company.

Kenny Fried is contributing author to Chapter 7. Kenny's dynamic approach to special events such as festivals, fairs, golf tournaments, and parades is known for its creativity and originality.

Sonoko Tatsukami, whose organizational and computer skills were instrumental in formatting the manuscript and juggling thousands of passages into logical sequences. Her research efforts were tireless and precise, and her good cheer a continuous boost to us all.

A Special Bow To

Jay Lurye, the late, but original event guru. In the 1970s, his creative concepts in event production, staging, and promotion gave birth to a new genre of unique approaches to the art. He dragged me and my young peers kicking and screaming as he showed us imaginative ways of making the old new and transforming the mundane into the memorable. With considerable trepidation, we followed.

As we grew in the profession, we found ourselves teaching and practicing his concepts (because we discovered, to our dismay, that they actually worked). His marketing skills emphasized the surprise factor, and the masses came to see what new delights awaited them. He made almost as many enemies as friends (his demands drove hoteliers and suppliers to distraction, but when the smoke cleared they would usually revel in the success of the event and the enthusiastic crowds that they drew). Whether a detractor or a disciple, no one could deny his creative genius.

Even today, I recognize his touch and his early contributions in every event industry seminar I attend and book I read. You will rarely hear his name anymore, but you will benefit from his work.

His challenges to the industry were daunting, but the results were exhilarating. I love him still.

Acknowledgments

There is no single, definitive instruction manual in the glove compartment of the event marketing vehicle. In reality, there are thousands of such manuals, each building on the books of knowledge that preceded them and adding to the bodies of knowledge that will fill the stream of future information.

I am blessed to have been associated with the best of the best during my career. Among my mentors are scholars, marketers, managers, writers, educators, financial analysts, researchers, association and corporate executives, producers, and attorneys. Yet they have a striking commonality. They have expertise in all disciplines of the events industry: marketing and management of special events, conventions, expositions, corporate meetings, tours, fundraisers, international study missions, educational symposia ad infinitum. And in so doing, they maintain the health and welfare of the organizations that sponsor these events. Every one of these disciplines required one universal skill. Someone had to sell an idea, and then sell an event.

They are consummate professionals who have contributed directly to this text or counseled me in its development and encouraged me to pursue the project. Others are those whose influences through time molded my approach to event marketing and my appreciation for the priceless satisfaction one receives from bringing people together to learn, solve problems, make progress, advance industries and professions, and have some fun.

They have taught me all I know in this industry, through their writings, their teachings, their counsel, their actions, and their friendships. The eagerness to open one's mind to the wisdom of others is synergistic. It leads to a journey of countless directions, with each turn in the road leading to new revelations, questions, answers, and understanding.

The following list represents those pioneers, contemporaries, and colleagues who have personally enriched my understanding of event marketing. I have learned at their elbows. I have shared countless event war stories with them, all of which get better with each telling. I have been with them during both triumphs and trials and I have learned from it all. Because of them, I am able to share with you, through this book, some of the body of knowledge in event marketing that these relationships have gifted to me. These are the true authors; it is they who are still doing their teaching on these pages and telling their favorite stories. As you pursue this study, you will be enriched by their wisdom. And in turn and in your time, you will become the mentors of those who join you on the journey.

Edward H. Able, Jr.
Cynthia Albright
James Anderson, Esq.
Joe M. Baker, Jr., CAE
O. Gordon Banks, CAE
Donald E. Bender
Joseph Boehret
Gail Brown
Michael Brunner, CAE
Barbara Byrd Keenan, CAE
Lincoln H. Colby, CMP
Thomas Connellan, Ph.D.
Alice Conway, MM, CSEP
Jill Cornish, IOM
Timothy Cunningham
James R. Daggett, CAE, CMP
John Jay Daly

J. Franklyn Dickson, CMP
David Dorf, CHME
David Dubois, CAE
Joan Eisenstodt
Sara Elliott
Roy B. Evans, Jr., CAE
Duncan Farrell, CMP
Howard Feiertag, CHA, CHME, CMP
Rose Folsom
John Foster III, Esq., CAE
Kenny Fried
LaRue Frye, CMP
Robert A. Gilbert, CHME
Joe Goldblatt, CSEP
Glenn Graham, CHME
Richard Green

Edwin L. Griffin, Jr., CAE
Leon J. Gross, Ph.D.
Earl C. Hargrove, Jr.
Marilyn Hauck, CMP
Donald E. Hawkins, Ph.D.
Anne Daly Heller
Ross E. Heller
Kenneth Hine, CHA
Jonathan T. Howe, Esq.
Judy Hoyle
Bernard J. Imming, CAE
Thomas J. A. Jones
Finiana Joseph
Bill Just, CAE, CMP
Walter M. Kardy
David C. King
Jeffrey W. King, Esq.
George D. Kirkland, CAE
William Knight
Thomas Knowlton, CHME
Gary A. LaBranche, CAE
Amy A. Ledoux, CMP
Hugh K. Lee
Sammy Little
Vance Lockhart, CAE
Cornelius R. Love III
James P. Low, CAE
Jay Lurye
Sandi Lynn, CMP
Joan Machinchick
Dawn M. Mancuso, CAE
Thomas T. McCarthy,
  CHMA
Linda R. McKinney
John F. Metcalfe
Caren Milman
Charles M. Mortensen, CAE

Lawrence P. Mutter
Jill Norvell
Mary Lou O'Brian
Michael Olson, CAE
Neil Ostergren, CHME
Nikolaj M. Petrovic, CAE
Adrian Phillips, CHME
Paul Radde, Ph.D.
Alan T. Rains, Jr.
Priscilla Richardson
Julia Rutherford-Silvers, CSEP
Susan Sarfati, CAE
Peter Shure
Robert H. Steel, CAE
Debbie Stratton
Martin L. Taylor
Jerry Teplitz, J.D., Ph.D.
Charles Ticho
James Tierney, CHME
Erin Turner
Sylvia van Laar
Jack J. Vaughn, CHA
John C. Vickerman
Scott Ward
George D. Webster, Esq.
Ilsa Whittemore
Jack Withiam, Esq.
DeWayne Woodring, CMP
Charles L. Wrye
Jill Zeigenfus
Ron Zemke
George Washington University,
Event Management Certificate
Program
Johnson & Wales University,
Alan Shawn Feinstein
Graduate School

Event Marketing

CHAPTER 1

Introduction to Event Marketing

No Great Thing Is Created Suddenly

—Epictetus (ca. 50–120)

WHEN YOU HAVE COMPLETED THIS CHAPTER, YOU WILL BE ABLE TO:

- Identify some of the pioneers of event marketing
- Understand the evolution of event marketing as practiced by associations and professional societies
- Appreciate the basics of integrative marketing in order to capture the optimum audiences available to you

---

History is rich with examples of creative geniuses who have dreamed beyond the borders of the conventional in order to develop awareness and increase sales for their events. We can learn much from their unique and sometimes outrageous stunts and attractions. While their venues and ventures were very different, they all shared a commonality of purpose, namely, the three *Es of event marketing:*

- Entertainment
- Excitement
- Enterprise

Whether you are marketing a complete convention or a stand-alone awards banquet, all three of these elements are critical to the continuing success of any event. *Entertainment,* for example, is available everywhere in our society. Years ago, people had to make a special effort to leave their homes to attend the theater or a sporting event to enjoy entertainment. They are now saturated with convenient home entertainment options on television, CDs and DVDs, computers, and videos. Key to your marketing success is the need to provide entertainment that will once again compel your audience to leave home to experience something they will not find there, because what you are offering is different, unique, and designed just for them.

Excitement may seem intangible, but it is real. It is key to making an event memorable. Excitement may be generated by entertainment that "blows the doors off the place": the great band, the dazzling magician, the fabulous party staged in the atrium lobby of a resort hotel. But entertainment may have nothing to do with the excitement promised by an event marketer. Many marketers miss the opportunity to promise excitement in other critical features of their meetings and other events.

Excitement can be part of a tribute to an industry leader, a new corporate logo introduced at a sales conference, or a celebration of an association's anniversary. The point is that it should always be considered as part of an effective marketing plan.

For example, the greatest excitement for an attendee may be the eye-opening revelations of that special educational program that advances knowledge and career opportunities and changes lives forever. Or it may be the impact of that keynote speaker whose motivational message will become a lasting asset, and cherished memory, for the listener. The lesson? In whatever you market, incorporate excitement as part of the promise. And then make sure it is delivered.

Enterprise is defined in *Webster's Unabridged Dictionary* as, among other things, a "readiness to take risks or try something untried; energy and initiative." If there is any characteristic that defines the pioneers in event marketing, it is that. The willingness to stretch the bounds of reason, to sail into uncharted waters, drove marketing's original landscapers into the imagination and conscience of the publics that they sought to attract.

> *What Would You Attempt to Do If You Knew You Could Not Fail?*

They understood the natural inclination of people to experience something new, to be among the first to be able to describe those experiences to their friends, and to become part of the inner sanctum of the new enterprise. They wanted to "blow the doors off the place" and dared to ask the impertinent questions.

Let's take a look at just a few of these marketing pioneers.

BILL VEECK

Bill Veeck was professional baseball's first promotional genius. As owner of the Cleveland Indians, Chicago White Sox, St. Louis Browns, and two minor league teams, he was a showman without peer. He understood that in the 1930s and 1940s, a country coming out of the depression and war years needed something more than the game on the field in order to spend precious dollars. They needed entertainment and excitement, and he was certainly committed to enterprise.

His greatest strength was his ability to determine what the fans wanted and were willing to pay for. He constantly mingled with spectators in his ballparks, prompting his son Mike to comment, "I think people looked at it as quaint, Dad sitting in the stands. It was just his way of doing *market research.*"

Veeck learned, for example, that many people in Chicago worked afternoons and nights in the factories and stockyards. So he scheduled a number of 8:30 A.M. starting times for games, attracting national attention when he personally served coffee and cornflakes to the early risers.

A visit to his ballpark offered constant surprises, including live music and dancers, giveaways of everything from lobsters to boxes of nails that he bartered from others, and the first "exploding scoreboard" where a home run by the home team ignited fireworks over the outfield fence. He planted the ivy on the outfield wall of

Wrigley Field in Chicago, which even today is a nationally recognized landmark of that facility.

But perhaps his most famous (or notorious, depending on your perspective) stunt occurred during his ownership of the Cleveland Indians. With much fanfare, he hired a midget to join the Indians. Eddie Gaedel stood 3 feet, 7 inches and weighed all of 65 pounds. When he was sent up to bat to draw a walk during a critical part of the game, the crowd went wild. The perplexed pitcher couldn't find the tiny strike zone and walked Gaedel on four pitches. Veeck claimed that this wasn't a stunt, but a "practical idea," which he would not hesitate to use again.

The president of the American League was not amused and barred Gaedel from playing again. But this unique marketing ploy certainly fulfilled the criteria of being memorable. Fifty years later, it is still an event that is memorialized by sports fans everywhere.

JAY LURYE

If there ever was a master of integrative marketing and creative thinking, it was Jay Lurye, the founder and president of Impact, International. Based in Chicago, his company was among the first event production and marketing firms, and many of his principles innovated practices that are common in the industry today. Much of his work centered on association conventions, but his greatest contributions were in building attendance through marketing partnerships and the creation of ancillary activities.

For example, Lurye instituted the spouse and youth program as a major part of the convention itself. He understood that if an organization could attract spouses by marketing unique programs to them and their children, chances were that the association's members would feel more compelled to register. He was right.

In marketing these programs, he was equally innovative. For example, Lurye created the "meet a celebrity" event and promoted the "mystery guest" luncheon or reception where spouses would buy tickets based on the promise that they would see not only each other, but mix with celebrities as well. Then, through his contacts with theatrical agents, he would determine which celebrities would be in town at the time of the event, hire them for a moderate fee to spend an hour socializing with the group, and watch as the spouses lined up for a chance to chat with the famous actress or singer. Photographers took Polaroid pictures as keepsakes, and autographs were traded. There are many companies today that hire "look-alike" celebrities to perform the same function, and it still works to build attendance and excitement. Jay Lurye started the concept, but he used the real McCoy!

He used his creativity and imagination to enlist "target markets" into the fold as "marketing partners." For example, the Mechanical Contractors Association of America was his client and was struggling to get support from its state and city chapters to attend the annual convention. Lurye's concept was to change the association's chapters from passive to active marketing partners. He would give them a proprietary interest in the enterprise.

So he created a major reception and dinner as a highlight of the convention and challenged the chapters to be among the first 20 to sponsor "hospitality centers" in which they would offer food and drink indigenous to their localities, giveaways of memorabilia, and costumed characters reminiscent of their state's history. Only 20 theme centers were available. First come, first served. They clamored to get on board.

Their pride swelling, the chapters immediately began trying to outdo each other. The Kansas City chapter proudly served barbecue and gave away miniature Kansas City Chiefs footballs. The Louisiana chapter served fried oysters and crawfish and tossed Mardi Gras doubloons and masks as a Dixieland band regaled the crowd. The Seattle chapter drew a crowd with its smoked salmon and Washington State wines. Seventeen other theme stations competed for attention. The party became a living, exciting montage of the association's width, breadth, and diversity.

But while the event was a marketing marvel and a great success, Lurye had a subtle strategy. The association itself saved a fortune on food and beverage expenses and entertainment costs that the sponsoring chapters covered, all of which would have fallen on the association for a more standard party.

In time, Lurye expanded his creativity into corporate meetings and product launches, and ultimately conceived a service company producing college and fraternal reunions with the same cutting-edge creativity he used to bring association events into the modern age. Many of his marketing and management principles still form the basis for contemporary event production and promotion.

P. T. BARNUM AND THE RINGLING BROTHERS

Phineas Taylor Barnum set the stage in the 1800s for using the outrageous and bizarre in attracting attention to his enterprises. He was responsible for developing methods of advertising and promotion that became known as *ballyhoo,* a term synonymous with attention getting. Businesses around the world, perhaps without realizing it, still employ his principles of entertainment, excitement, and enterprise. And they profit from it. Barnum created his own "stars" and then promoted them through advertising, flyers, and posters as he brought them to town. He was also a pioneer in the concept of public displays of his attractions, building his reputation and profits through museums and road shows. Among his feature attractions were General Tom Thumb (the world's smallest human), Jumbo (the world's largest elephant), and the golden-voiced Jenny Lind (the Swedish Nightingale), whom he introduced to American audiences with great fanfare in the 1850s.

It's interesting to note that his promotions left a permanent impression on the American lexicon. In addition to his Jumbo elephant attraction was a "genuine" white elephant named Toung Taloung. Barnum spent a fortune trying to convince audiences that Toung was not a fake, to little success. To this day, the term "jumbo" connotes bigness. And "white elephant" defines anything that is expensive to maintain, but yields little or no profitable results.

He and his partner, James A. Bailey, took his menagerie on the road, combining the wild animals with other circus acts. They were convinced that success lay in taking the enterprise to the people rather than waiting for audiences to find their "Greatest Show on Earth." The partners took this approach to a fine art of promotion and marketing after merging with the Ringling Brothers Circus in 1919. They built circus wagons for the tour, gaily painted with promises of amazing feats and attractions. In time, they began loading their wagons onto railway cars and then began purchasing freight cars themselves, again painting them in bold colors so no one could mistake the fact that the circus was coming.

Barnum and Bailey were already practicing target marketing, although the term had not been invented at that time. They knew that the communities their show visited needed to know that entertainment was on the way, that excitement was right around the bend!

Thus began the marketing techniques that Ringling Bros. and Barnum & Bailey practices today: publishing a road schedule, sending advance press releases to pertinent media sources, and announcing the exact train schedule so that people could gather with their "children of all ages" at train stations along the route to watch the circus cars roar by. Their target markets were not just the destination cities but also the public at large.

They included every town en route. Today, you can find Web sites with photos posted by people who take pictures of the train as it passes through their communities; such is the power of imaginative target marketing. People who could not attend the circus performing miles away could at least be a part of it as it graced their town by just passing through. This was a brilliant marketing strategy, designed to attract national attention despite the fact that it was essentially a product that was offered locally. And then, to gain even more publicity, their producers staged a parade from the train station to the circus site, bringing throngs to see the animals, costumed performers, and clowns up close—even before the first tent had been erected. To this day, this combination of street "stunts" and parades attracts the attention of millions, most of whom cannot attend the event itself.

In many ways, the theories that the Ringling Brothers and P. T. Barnum began developing in the 1800s are even more effective today. Never could they have dreamed of the new technologies that we take for granted, making even more productive the marketing concepts they practiced then—entertainment, excitement, and enterprise, and an understanding of target markets. This marketing strategy quilts a fabric of awareness not just on show site but throughout the countryside, and creates a warm and fuzzy consciousness of earlier, more carefree times.

And that is what P. T. Barnum and the Ringling Brothers had in mind in the first place.

GEORGE PRESTON MARSHALL

Marketing genius is found in those who take fledgling enterprises and through innovation and customer involvement build hugely successful products. George Preston Marshall was such a marketer.

In 1937, he purchased the old Boston Redskins professional

football team and moved the franchise to Washington, DC, renaming it the Washington Redskins. In those days, professional football was more of a curiosity than serious sport. Baseball was the national pastime. Football was something to do on a cold Sunday afternoon with no great import or urgency.

Marshall was a master showman, and he surrounded himself with others who shared his vision. He realized that to build a fan base, he needed to offer more than punts and passes on the field. He needed to offer entertainment, excitement, and enterprise. He began by asking the impertinent question: What can we do to build "traditions" that our fans will take to their hearts, when last year they didn't even have a team to root for?

Through songwriter Barnee Breeskin, the conductor of the orchestra at Washington's Shoreham Hotel, Marshall produced a fight song, the first for a professional football team. Breeskin's opus was originally called the "Washington Redskins March." Today, it is known throughout the United States as "Hail to the Redskins!"

It became the rallying cry as crowds grew from the hundreds to the thousands, singing the song not just in the stadium but also on the streets and in bars and taverns as the popularity of the team grew. It is still a staple of the football franchise, sung by the crowd after every Redskin touchdown and field goal more than 60 years later, a lasting marketing medium.

Marshall also realized that he needed an instrument to capitalize on the new anthem. He collaborated once again with Breeskin, beginning with Breeskin's swing band and transforming the enterprise into a full-fledged marching band. The Redskins Marching Band became the first in professional football.

In his marketing mind, Marshall realized that this was not just about entertainment. It was also about creating awareness and building attendance. The band became a staple throughout the region, performing not just in the Washington, DC, area but also throughout the South where no competition for professional football franchises existed. The customer/fan base throughout Virginia, the Carolinas, and as far south as Georgia expanded dramatically.

There were times when the musical entertainment was more compelling than the game itself. It is often credited with quadrupling the attendance in the first three years of the team's existence in Washington, DC.

Fabulous pregame and halftime shows drew the crowds more than the team's on-field performance, some suspected. Columnist Bob Considine described it this way: "A Redskins game is something resembling a fast-moving revue, with cues, settings, music, pace, tableaux and, hold your hats, boys, a ballet. The amazing part of it all is that there's room left on the program for a football game!" Marshall was marketing his team as all-encompassing entertainment on a Sunday afternoon, not just a football game. He was drawing families, not just fans. A football game at old Griffith Stadium became an *event*. Football was just an integral part of the celebration.

Yet another example of Marshall's brilliance in producing stunts and promoting his product was the annual arrival of Santa Claus at the game scheduled just before Christmas. There was nothing new about Santa Claus making an appearance at a game during the holidays. That was done all the time, throughout the country. In Washington, DC, however, it was *how* Santa arrived that captured the imagination of Marshall's audiences. Each year, speculation began in the newspapers and on radio broadcasts. People bought tickets early to make certain they were among the privileged who personally would witness the arrival of Santa Claus.

Under Marshall's creative guidance, Santa arrived in every way imaginable. Through the years, he has entered the halftime show amid great fanfare by sleigh, by parachute, on horseback, and tethered to a wire strung from the top of the stadium. In more recent years, a helicopter has landed with Santa at midfield, and he has even "materialized" through magical illusions. It remains a staple of the team's tradition and Christmas entertainment.

As with any business, in the professional football industry that Marshall helped create years ago, a few Super Bowls and other successes certainly help sell tickets. But the foundation of any enterprise is the building of *brand recognition* and a faithful following in good times and bad. George Preston Marshall recognized that football wins and losses would come and go, but entertainment and excitement would attract customers forever.

The Evolution of Conventions and Conferences: The Role of Associations

With this understanding of the pioneers of event marketing, we must recognize trade associations and professional societies, which provide the structures that nurture such events. These organizations have played a vital role in the evolution of conferences, expositions, and conventions.

The dictionary defines an association as an "organization of persons having a common interest." Since the Middle Ages and the European guild system, associations have been giving people a reason to congregate for mutual interests and purposes.

In other words, associations are incubators for events of all types, serving the myriad purposes for which associations exist. Among the functions of associations are

- Establishing industry standards
- Influencing legislative/political affairs
- Improving employee/employer relations
- Building a body of knowledge through publications
- Defining the industry/profession through demographics
- Providing greater purchasing power through group discounts
- Disseminating general information
- Creating and maintaining social relationships
- Performing public service activities
- Developing statistical data and research
- Expanding members' professional development
- Offering education and training
- Providing group travel opportunities
- Creating positive public relations
- Handling industry/professional legal affairs
- Identifying and defining common causes
- Introducing opportunities for entertainment, networking, and peer interaction

These are just some of the functions performed by associations and professional societies. And when you examine each function, you will find opportunities to hold events, along with jobs for those who market these events (see Figure 1-1).

More than any other institution, associations have driven the definition and identification of event marketing as a profession.

Sampling of Association Events

- Conventions
- Expositions
- Seminars
- Board and committee meetings
- Awards presentations
- Celebrations and anniversaries
- Community service events
- Symposia
- Educational and video conferences
- Presentation of papers
- Receptions
- Sport and recreation programs
- Political rallies
- Installation of officers/leaders
- Tours and study missions
- Training programs

Figure 1-1
These types of events are marketed by most associations to their members and supporters. Many additional event types may be produced, based on the specific disciplines of each association.

Gone are the days when association events were simply seen as crowds of conventioneers reveling through hotel lobbies wearing funny hats and tossing water balloons. Today, associations and professional societies consider their events the most critical functions they provide because the gathering of members of any event must fulfill a defined purpose and personify the corporate culture of the association. Marketers have learned that the competition for members' time and dollars is too great to do otherwise.

Event marketing has been transformed from an organizational afterthought to a professional discipline upon which the association depends for its very livelihood. And the association community, more than any other entity, has guided other types of event planners toward innovative and creative ways of attracting participation and the greatest byproduct—public awareness.

Corporate meetings, religious retreats, civic celebrations, reunions, sporting events, fundraisers, technical and scientific symposia, product introductions, parades, awards, and honors dinners—all have benefited from the principles of event marketing begun by the pioneers of the art such as those described earlier and refined by the legions of association practitioners who have followed.

Regardless of the nature of the event, its success will depend on the recognition by the event marketer that the *five Ps* of marketing will play an essential role.

The Five Ps of Event Marketing

1. Product
2. Price
3. Place
4. Public Relations
5. Positioning

1. PRODUCT

The successful event marketer is at first the consummate student of his or her product. The product may be an educational program, a county fair, or a full-fledged convention. It may be a reunion for a fraternal organization or a corporate product launch. If you are marketing the event, there are essential elements as shown in Figure 1-4 that you must know and questions you must ask of the event sponsor.

1. What Is the History of the Event? Many veteran marketers will attract participation because they can sell the celebratory essence of the event. "The 50th Annual Conference" proclaims the success and venerability of an organization, as well as the pride that goes with being part of it. But even if there is no history, there is the opportunity to be historical. For example, "The 1st Annual Conference" will have no history, but can be portrayed as an opportunity to get in on the ground floor of a "happening" that participants can infer will be an ongoing event, turning into a tradition and developing long-term loyalty. The greatest part of event marketing is the opportunity to create history, by attracting people into a synergistic activity that can define the organization and its goals.

A major association recently celebrated its 10th Annual Educational Conference. The event marketer positioned his promotion with the theme "The Power of 10." *Ten* major prizes were to be awarded. The *10* top-ranking speakers from previous years were to be invited back to present seminars and to be honored at a general session. *Ten* lucky attendees would be presented with complimentary registration for next year's event. And so on. The simple concept of 10 years of success was themed throughout the marketing mix. The celebration of history is a fabulous promotional asset in whatever way the event marketer wishes to interpret it for the audience.

2. What Is the Value of the Product? Marketing an event requires that the message emphasizes the manner in which the participant will benefit. The promise of increasing productivity, maximizing profitability, or simply having a great time can be legitimate benefits that can persuade a person to buy the product or attend the event. Later in this text, we will discuss the science of studying demographics and determining audience needs. Designing an event with that research in hand and effectively describing how that event will fulfill those needs are keys to effective marketing.

3. What Makes the Product Unique? What makes this event different from others? Why should one choose to invest time and money in this event, as opposed to the competition that surrounds it? Marketers that can identify the return on investment (ROI) that can be expected by the participants, the special experience that will be offered, and the added value of attendance are those who will successfully market the event. This will require research into the markets and into the objectives of the client or organization. Only then can the uniqueness of the product be identified and described in all of the marketing media utilized.

2. PRICE

Primary among the responsibilities of the event marketer is an understanding of the financial goals of the sponsoring organization. Once this is determined, market research will illustrate the competition's pricing patterns: Who is offering a similar product, to whom, and at what price? Equally important are considerations such as the level of demand for the product and economic indicators such as the relative health of the economy in a particular city or region or, to an increasing extent, globally.

Price may be secondary to *perceived value*. It is in this area that the event marketer can play a major role.

In marketing events, consider these issues of pricing:

What Is the Corporate Financial Philosophy? Some events are designed to make money, pure and simple. Others are strategically developed to break even financially. And there

Perceived Value: A Small-Town Story

In the summertime in the small town of Gaithersburg, Maryland, school was out but the high school band members wanted to stay in tune. So they organized a summer concert to be held in the gym. Between practices for the performance, they distributed flyers around town advertising "Celebrate Summer at a FREE CONCERT at the High School." The night of the concert came, but only a handful of parents showed up. Although the music was adequate, the attendance was awful. It was a dismal failure.

Undaunted, the band tried again. They stumbled on another marketing principle that, in essence, says, "You get what you pay for." This time, the promotional flyers were distributed saying "Celebrate Summer at this SPECIAL PERFORMANCE of the Mighty Sounds of the Gaithersburg High School Band. Only $5 for Adults, $2.50 for Students, Children under 10, Free. Limited Seating! Don't Be Left Out!"

The performance sold out. The band held three more concerts before the summer was over. And from the proceeds, they were able to purchase new uniforms. Perceived value was indeed a product of pricing.

are some that are positioned as "loss leaders," expected to lose money in an effort to gain greater assets elsewhere, such as membership development or community goodwill. Corporate meetings are typically expensed not as profit centers but rather as "costs of doing business" in order to build employee loyalty and pride and to learn how better to sell products and services. The event marketer must clearly understand the financial mission and design a strategy to accommodate those goals.

What Is the Cost of Doing Business? Price must reflect the total costs of goods and services, *including* the cost of marketing itself. Marketing is often relegated to a secondary role in event production because the costs of printing, postage, advertising, public relations, and other basic marketing expenses may not be considered part of the event budget. Instead, it may be treated as part of the organization's general overhead and operating expenses. The marketer will be considered an integral part of event production when that event's budget provides for marketing as a primary event function and income-expense center.

What Are the Financial Demographics of the Target Audience? Analyze your market's ability to pay. This sounds simple, but it is critical to the marketing effort. An event designed for executives who have access to corporate credit cards and can charge their participation as business expenses will likely be priced at a higher level than an event designed for those who must pay from their own personal wallets. Market research will help determine the ability and willingness of attendees to pay ticket prices at various levels and, therefore, influence the planning of the event itself.

3. PLACE

In the real estate industry, the old saying about ascertaining the value of a property is "location, location, location." The same is said in the hospitality industry when planners decide where to buy or build new facilities. It is no less true when marketing an event. The location of your event can dictate not just the attendance, but the character and personality of the event as well. This is a consideration for the earliest part of the planning stages.

For example, for an event being held at a plush resort, the setting for the event should be a key part of the marketing strategy. The event site may even be the major draw featured in brochures and advertising. An awards dinner at a new public facility in your town should emphasize the opportunity to experience the facility as an exciting highlight of the event itself.

On the other hand, an educational seminar at an airport hotel would not necessarily feature the attractiveness of the site but rather could emphasize the convenience and functionality of the location as the major asset for the attendee. Place should be marketed with a number of important elements in mind as shown in Figure 1-2.

1. Proximity to the potential attendees and ease of travel
2. Availability of parking for a commuter audience
3. Ambiance and originality of the site
4. Logistical practicality of staging a particular event
5. Surrounding attractions/infrastructure for ancillary activities
6. Existence of related audiences, organizations
7. Degree to which the location fits the character of the event
8. Safety, security of event attendees
9. Availability of public transportation (airport and city)
10. Availability of overflow space (sleeping and meeting rooms)

Figure 1-2
The decision to choose a location is based on more than the appearance of the facility. Selection must be made with the audience and its profile in mind.

4. PUBLIC RELATIONS

Public relations is a major part of the marketing mix. You can advertise anything you want—that is, what you say about your organization and your event. Public relations can determine what *others* perceive of you and your mission. It may be as bold as a team of press agents distributing releases to newspapers or staging press conferences to extol the virtues of your event. Or it may be as subtle as a trade publication interview with a leader of your organization, when the interview includes references to your event and its benefits. The essence of a public relations campaign is that it never stops; rather, it is an ongoing effort to establish positive perceptions of your organization and its products.

The first step in establishing a public relations campaign is to determine what the current perception is. The patriarch of modern public relations is Edward Bernays, the namesake of the most revered public relations award in the hospitality industry (the annual Bernays Award sponsored by the Hospitality Sales and Marketing Association International). Bernays was a devotee of research, the need to survey, to conduct focus groups with facilitators, and to thoroughly research the attitudes and needs of target markets. He also initiated methods of matching the marketing strategies with those professed needs. Bernays advocated the need to maintain the research effort continuously, to detect changing attitudes and to remain current in meeting and fulfilling them.

You need not be a public relations professional to practice effective public relations. A media release, feature article, or simple phone call to the editor of a trade publication can result in invaluable publicity for your event. Most industry publications and newspapers welcome these materials, which they use as "fillers," but which appear as news articles. That insert will build the credibility of not only your event, but also your organization. And it's free!

The information you provide to a news source must be "slanted," however, to reflect a news style rather than an advertising tone. For example, if you approach a publication with the fact that you are holding an industry conference, you will probably be told to "buy an ad." But if your message is that major new economic and legislative initiatives will be developed during your general session, the results of which may change the direction of the industry, your chances of getting "ink" are much greater. You may be asked to submit an article or provide more details. You may also find a reporter in the general session to write a follow-up article or editorial covering the proceedings.

There is an old—somewhat cynical—saying: "I don't care what you say about me; just spell my name right." This urges caution. You must care what people say, and your message to the public must be carefully crafted to reflect the character and strategy of your event.

The effective event marketer will seize on every opportunity to plant the seeds of credibility and positive response. For example, the American Society of Association Executives stages a community project as an ancillary activity during its convention. Wherever the association convenes, volunteer attendees are enlisted to go into the community; grab paint cans, hammers and nails, rakes and brooms; and rehabilitate a playground or a building. Not only is this attractive to local newspapers and television and radio stations, pictures and stories of this goodwill effort appear throughout professional journals. The positive results are priceless. Therefore, the convention itself becomes a platform for expanded credibility, goodwill, publicity, and far-reaching recognition of the association.

Can one put a dollar value on public relations? Perhaps one can, although placing a definitive value on the results may be

---

Tools of the Trade in Event Public Relations

- Media releases (news oriented)
- Publicity releases (promotionally oriented)
- Media kits (including photographs, biographies, press releases, brochures, organizational fact sheets, schedules, speakers' backgrounds and topics, mission statements, ancillary activities)
- Phone, fax, and e-mail information for contacts
- Radio and TV spots/releases
- Copies of speeches
- Videotapes
- Audiotapes
- Invitations/tickets to event

Figure 1-3
These tried-and-true public relations vehicles are designed to develop the message and deliver it to as many audiences as possible.

problematical. The Public Relations Society of America estimates that the value of editorial coverage is three times greater than the cost of a purchased advertisement of equal size and space.

In his book, *Guerrilla Marketing,* Jay Conrad Levinson makes a compelling argument as to the value of public relations, because he was able to absolutely track it. He was purchasing advertising to sell a self-published book. Each $1,000 ad generated some $3,000 in book sales. A reporter from his hometown newspaper read the book and found it fascinating. He called Levinson to ask if he could interview him and bring along a photographer. After the interview and subsequent news article (which did not directly solicit sales of the book), more than $10,000 in sales resulted almost immediately. Levinson wrote ". . . and the marketing didn't cost me one penny."

Figure 1-3 illustrates classic public relations devices.

5. POSITIONING

Event marketing relies on the proper positioning of the product. No event can be effectively sold until a marketing plan is developed. The marketing plan will likely be the predicate that determines success or failure. And the key to a successful marketing plan is "positioning."

Positioning is the strategy of determining, through intuition, research, and evaluation, those areas of consumer need that your event can fulfill. What types of events is the competition offering? What level of investment are they requiring of their attendees? Who is attending, and who is not? In other words: *What niche are we trying to fill?* What makes us *different* and how can we seize upon our unique qualities to market our events? And what markets will be receptive to our event concept? The event marketing executive who can answer these questions has the greatest opportunity of fulfilling expectations. Here are some key considerations when positioning an event.

LOCATION

In previous events, is the East Coast being favored, leaving a niche opportunity on the West Coast? Is a regional event in the habit of serving the downtown constituencies while disenfranchising those in the rural areas? Do we always meet in a hotel ballroom, when a change-of-pace venue such as a museum or amusement park may attract new interest and attendance? Issues of location must be continuously evaluated, because interests of the markets change constantly.

ATTENTION SPAN

People forget quickly. Studies have shown that people are bombarded with some 2,700 messages daily. In the midst of all that information, establishing the position of an event is a daunting task. Marketing materials must constantly emphasize the needs the event will satisfy and the benefits it will provide, because potential attendees will likely be thinking about a thousand other things.

COMPETITIVE COSTS

When positioning an event, a prime consideration is the cost of admission. What level of registration fee is the competition charging? What level of success are they experiencing? Positioning strategies must consider the economic level and flexibility of the audience being sought, and meet that expectation. Some organizations hold events where admission is free (because of limited resources of the attendees) and the costs are covered by exhibitors, sponsors, and supporters. Others may set the cost of participation exceedingly high in order to attract only the market niche represented by big spenders and industry leaders. There is no one definitive answer, other than that registration/participation fee issues are a significant part of correctly positioning the event and an integral cog in the marketing plan.

PROGRAM

What can you offer in your event program that no one else is offering and, consequently, market the uniqueness? You may find an opportunity to honor an industry or community leader. There may be an educational segment that can be featured or an "open forum"

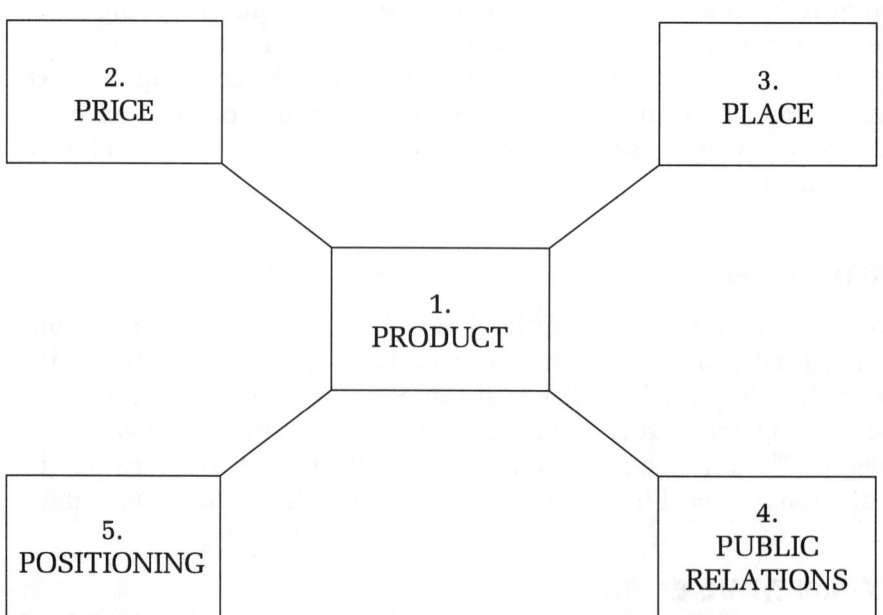

Figure 1-4
Only when the product is clearly defined can decisions be made as to strategies to be used in attracting audiences through price, place, positioning, and public relations.

debate designed to explore the future of the group or industry. Uniqueness in programming is essential to marketing success; "sameness" is lethal in the long run.

KEEP IT SIMPLE

The more complex the positioning considerations, the more complex the marketing plan will likely be. The more daunting the marketing plan, the less likely you will be able to follow it faithfully. The plan should simply spell out, as briefly as feasible, the strengths and weaknesses of your organization and event, the objectives, the needs of your potential market niche, economic considerations, and elements that will make the enterprise unique from others. Short and sweet. And easy to track.

Research and Analysis

We learned earlier that a key component of the five Ps of marketing is market research and analysis. Before one can effectively design and market an event, there is the need to determine the desires, expectations, and anticipations of the audience to whom that marketing will be directed. The event may be an original production—or a historic, traditional annual meeting—but research must be ongoing.

Studies have shown that 30 percent of Americans move each year, either from their homes or from their jobs. Therefore, because people change, expectations change. And so markets change. Markets must be segmented in order to apply emphasis to those who are most important. Organizations will have primary, or target, markets, the mainstream of their constituencies and memberships. However, many have found additional participants through examination of secondary and tertiary markets. This may extend far beyond the mainstream markets to suppliers, sponsors, and ancillary providers. The search for new markets should never cease. It is imperative to research them all because that research may show that a tertiary market may be more financially lucrative than the primary audience for which the event is designed.

For example, many conventions are assembled to serve the common business concerns of association members through business sessions and educational programs. Yet the events are made feasible primarily through the financial and personal support of those who sell products and services to the primary members. These supporters are most often exhibitors, sponsors, and advertisers. While not the primary market for the convention, they form a critically important secondary market. And because of their financial support and influence, their opinions and attitudes are equally vital and determinable through research of the secondary market they compose.

By researching markets in depth, the event marketer will be able to spot trends in time to respond to changing needs as well as to resolve small problems before they become major ones. As demographics, desires, and issues change, marketing must be on pace with change to address those market fluctuations in all available promotional media and marketing vehicles.

QUANTITATIVE/QUALITATIVE RESEARCH

There are two basic categories of research instruments with which we should be familiar: quantitative and qualitative surveys. Either can be considered for both preevent and postevent research. And qualitative methodology is extremely effective during the event itself.

The major difference between the two is this: *Quantitative* research allows little room for interpretation; it is a snapshot of attitude or opinion based on numerical or analytical ratings systems. It is typically faster because it is easy to execute and tabulate, less expensive, and not as open to conjecture as qualitative research instruments. On the other hand, *qualitative* research is more in depth, a study of opinions, objectives, visions, and experiential and performance observations. It is more time consuming, often more expensive, and more interpretive than the quantitative approach.

Again, both are often used simultaneously, as well as separately, and can be effective for preevent marketing and planning strategies as well as postevent evaluations. You will need to determine which may be the best method, given your timing, group characteristics, and type of information needed.

QUANTITATIVE RESEARCH (HARD DATA)

In most cases, this research is conducted on paper, electronically such as Internet applications, or through telemarketing. For example, assume you are considering two keynote speakers for your

Mid-Year Event. In your preevent quantitative research instrument, you ask your potential audience to rate which speaker they wish to hear, on a scale of 1 to 10 (1 being the lowest desirability; 10, the highest). Speaker A receives an average of 5.6 in your responses. Speaker B nails a 9.3.

This result needs little interpretation. The data are "hard." Go for speaker B, or be ready to explain the alternative! This system works well for all aspects of event marketing and evaluation, including the ratings of multiple educational programs, social events, and overall experiential responses. Quantitative research instruments are *objective*.

Questions may be developed in two different styles: In Figure 1-5, you will find a model of a typical quantitative preevent survey. This survey model is featured in Joe Goldblatt's text, *Best Practices in Modern Event Management,* 2nd ed. Two different styles of research items are used: Question 4 in this model uses a *Likert scale* to provide the opportunity for the respondent to precisely state his or her opinion. No room for maneuvering, or for interpretive flexibility. Question 5 allows some room for maneuvering in the answer, through the *semantic differential scale* technique.

As Dr. Goldblatt describes it in his text, the semantic differential scale style of question is used to "allow the respondent to respond by selecting a continuum between two opposing adjectives." In other words, there is a little more "wiggle room" (or perhaps "analytical interpretation" would be more appropriate terminology) for both the respondent and the researcher. Regardless, the results will provide a level of both demographic and psychographic data.

QUALITATIVE RESEARCH (SOFT DATA)

What's the hidden meaning? What are the objectives of this event? What are the ranges of interests in the markets we are trying to attract? These are the kinds of questions that compel qualitative research, the probing inspection of attitudes, opinions, interests, and organizational directions. By its nature, this type of research is more time consuming and expensive, as well as more open to varied and sometimes conflicting interpretation by analysts. Qualitative research instruments are *subjective*.

But qualitative research can be much more exciting! It's the "risk-taker research" if you are not afraid of what the answers may be. In other words, the results of qualitative techniques can take you to places you may not have thought of, lead you to fresh new concepts, perhaps all the way to the "Field of Dreams."

There are several favored ways to conduct qualitative research.

Focus Group

This is a small group of participants who are interested in the subject but who represent disparate representations of your market or constituency. They should have knowledge of the subject under

---

Quantitative Preevent Survey Model

The following survey will enable the organizers of XYZ event to determine the feasibility of producing the following event. Your participation is important in this effort. Answer all questions by checking the appropriate box. Return this survey by January 1, 2003.

1. Gender? ☐ Male ☐ Female

2. Age? ☐ Under 25 ☐ 26–34 ☐ 35–44 ☐ 45–60 ☐ 61 and over

3. Income? ☐ Under $24,999 ☐ $25,000–34,999 ☐ Over $35,000

4. If the event held during the summer I would: *(Likert scale)*
   ☐ Not Attend ☐ Maybe Attend ☐ No Opinion ☐ Probably Attend
   ☐ Positively Attend

5. If the event were held during the fall I would: *(semantic differential scale)*
   Not Attend ☐ 1 ☐ 2 ☐ 3 ☐ 4 ☐ 5 Positively Attend

6. If you checked number 1 above please describe your reasons for nonattendance in the space below: *(Open-ended question)*

_____

_____

_____

Return this survey by January 1, 2003 to:

Mary Event Manager
P.O. Box 14
Anywhere, USA

To receive a *free copy* of the survey results please include your business card.

Figure 1-5

The survey model in Figure 1-5 is primarily *quantitative*.
However, question 6 adds the possibility for a *qualitative* interpretation of an expanded response.

investigation, but not necessarily have been direct participants in the event being studied or even users of your product. The reasons they *do not* participate may be more enlightening than the reasons others do. In a relaxed atmosphere without the distractions of telephones or entertainment, the group focuses on your issues under the guidance of a *facilitator*.

The facilitator must also have knowledge of the topic in question, but should enter without a preconceived agenda or objective. Rather, the facilitator is responsible for keeping the discussions on topic, maintaining order, and deriving conclusions, whatever they may be. Recording of the discussions is often done with videotapes, audiotapes, or, at the very least, written transcriptions and flipchart notes.

The focus group deliberations may take an hour or a day, depending on the extent and complexity of the issues. The important point here is that plenty of time should be allowed for the objectives to be accomplished. The pressure of the clock is the greatest threat to generating thoughtful deliberations and meaningful consensus.

Observation/Participation

This research strategy requires alertness, consumption of time, and human interaction. For example, as a marketer of an event, you may want to visit the prospective venue to get a "feel for the place" in order to more graphically describe it in your marketing materials. Casual discussions with employees or locals will be effective gauges of the degree of interest in your event. Simply observing the levels of service being provided may directly improve the planning process by identifying potential problems that may be avoided for your event. How long is the line at the registration desk? How easy, or difficult, is it to park a car? How crowded is the coffee shop at the height of the breakfast hour? What are the general attitudinal levels of the staff and the quality of their service? What are the standards of housekeeping and the condition of the physical plant and surroundings? Become the detective. Scrutinize everything. Copious note taking and laser alertness are essential during this process.

While managing and marketing a major national convention, I would take time to visit every seminar room, a total of 65 seminars during a three-day period. I would count heads and compare the total to the total room capacity. I would observe the body language of the students and the teachers. Hands in the air were good. Heads on the table were bad. After a few informal exit interviews, I took my notes.

This was not rocket science, but it was an incredible asset when selecting topics, teachers, and room sizes the following year, making the adjustments mandated by my notes and marketing a more memorable event next time. This was the observation/participation technique at its most basic and most effective level.

Conducting Case Studies

An evaluation of comparable events that have preceded your project may provide unique insight into the marketing approach to an event. Investigation should include only similar types of events or products that have been produced by others and should delve into the relative success or failure and reasons why for each. Interviews, whether personally or electronically conducted, may provide clues to the strengths and weaknesses of the enterprise, determine whether or not it is competitive, and reveal those elements that should be emulated or avoided.

Key to this approach is comparability. The project, event, or product being examined must fit the mold of the one being considered so that the comparisons are valid. The researcher must be sensitive not only to the current success of the event being researched, but also to the historical data and trends in growth, composition, and participant demographics of that event. This will reveal the target markets and marketing techniques to be approached, or perhaps even rejected.

Summary

In this chapter, we have learned much from the pioneers of the event industry and their approaches to marketing. Many of their ideas are innovative even in today's modern markets. They knew the principles of the three Es and five Ps, and they knew what their markets wanted—perhaps even before their markets knew it. They took failed ideas in stride, exemplifying the old adage that "no opportunity is ever lost; the other person takes what you miss." Then they pressed on with more new concepts.

We also learned that "pricing," a major component of the five Ps, is not necessarily a matter of lower prices driving greater attendance at your event. The lessons learned about "perceived value" are noteworthy and practiced each day by experienced marketers. The key element in all of the considerations covered in this chapter is the research required to understand market needs and values. Quantitative and qualitative analysis techniques can be used separately or in tandem. But they must be used, continuously and creatively.

TALES FROM THE FRONT

A national association historically held an awards event as part of a breakfast program during its annual convention. The event was losing appeal, attendance was trending downward, and the honorees were less than pleased. The association employed qualitative interview research to determine what was wrong. The answer was simple. Many of the award recipients were from outside the association. Therefore, their peers were not attending the convention, and those that were attending did not feel that they were "stakeholders" in the event. In other words, other than the breakfast itself there was little compelling interest in the awards. It was the wrong market segment.

The research also showed that the awards event could be removed from the convention and reintroduced as a standalone, upscale black-tie dinner to be marketed to the industry at large. The key would be exclusivity—the "be there or be square" approach. The complexion of the marketing for the first event was "see and be seen." A small 200-person-capacity ballroom in a luxury downtown hotel was purposely selected for the first event under the assumption that the event would be easier to sell out and others who did not get their tickets ordered in time would be disappointed, frustrated, and would make certain that they were a part of the scene next year. The strategy: sacrifice a bit today and create the demand for the long term.

The strategy worked. The first event was elegantly small, tuxedos and ball gowns were on display, flashbulbs popped, and a new industry "happening" was born. In the postevent research that followed, the major complaint was "too crowded—you have to get a bigger room next year!" Now, if there was ever a "positive negative" for these marketing strategists, that is it.

That was 10 years ago. The association changed its marketing strategy to drop the "exclusivity" approach and moved the annual event to New York City, with greater ballroom space and increased industry representation to make attendance more convenient for the "movers and shakers" of the industry. Today, that event still attracts sell-outs, except that now it draws 800 attendees, rather than 200, and nets more than $250,000 for its coffers.

The lessons? The association used qualitative research techniques to find the source of the problem. It used the marketing technique of exclusivity to raise eyebrows and attract the attention of secondary markets within its industry. And its strategy of analyzing "place" as one of the key Ps of marketing was essential to accommodating incredible growth and industry awareness.

Chapter Challenge

You have been hired as an event marketing consultant by a state medical association. Your charge is to increase attendance and revenue and to create greater awareness of the organization in the medical community.

The association's conventions have been held in the same urban location for years, attendance is dwindling, and costs are rising. The convention is typically a two-day meeting, held over the weekend. Programming is heavy on technical symposia and light on social events. There is a small exposition, primarily open only during coffee breaks. There is no significant spouse participation or youth participation.

What marketing strategies would you consider to turn the organization's event around in terms of attendance and income?

CHAPTER 2

Event Promotion, Advertising, and Public Relations

Why Not Go Out on a Limb?
That's Where the Fruit Is.

—WILL ROGERS

WHEN YOU HAVE COMPLETED THIS CHAPTER, YOU WILL BE ABLE TO:

- Identify the five Ws of event marketing
- Determine the essential elements of an audience attitude questionnaire
- Understand the relationship between internal and external event marketing
- Determine marketing strategies that are essential to successful selling
- Compare relative values of public relations to advertising
- Identify the elements of a press release and a press kit

Event Promotion: Trends and Challenges

Regardless of the nature of your event, its success will largely depend on promotion. Promotion is vital in creating awareness of the event, a desire to participate, and a feeling by the potential participant that the investment of time and money validates the benefits the event offers.

As the economy and our society are transformed, we can identify many new challenges to our promotional strategies. Among them are:

Greater Competition

In 1996, there were 4,100 trade shows held annually in the United States, according to the Convention Industry Council (CIC). Four years later, the number of trade shows had increased to 4,600. Many of these were the result of spin-offs, duplicating national events with comparable regional events to attract more local and regional participants. National meetings are therefore becoming more "regional" in nature, accommodating the strictures of time, location, and economics faced by attendees.

The CIC study revealed that, 25 years ago, meetings attempting to attract a national attendance drew 36 percent of attendees from a radius of 200 miles or less. Today, the growing regionalization of these events is illustrated by the fact that more than 50 percent of attendees are drawn from this distance.

This trend is manifested by many sponsoring organizations and corporations that have "taken the show to the customer," rather than compete for long-distance attendees and the greater expenses attendant to both the sponsoring organization and the event guests and delegates.

This increasing abundance of meetings challenges your skills in advertising, direct mail, public relations, telemarketing, and electronic marketing to position your product as not only favorable, but also indispensable in the face of increasing alternatives for your potential attendees.

Costs of Travel and Accommodations

As we enter a new era of corporate mergers and turnovers in the hospitality and travel industry, we are seeing the costs of travel to certain locations increase.

For example, the clear trend is toward more hospitality properties owned and managed by fewer corporations, often lessening the flexibility of host properties to negotiate favorable rates and dates. The increase in airline mergers and the expansion of "hub" destinations have created the same scenario of higher rates, fewer destination/timing options for your guests, and more limited direct-travel service to certain destinations. These and other economic trends become major considerations in promotional positioning strategies. Marketing executives are increasingly sensitive to regionalization in their planning.

The dramatic growth in construction of event and meeting facilities, hotels, and conference centers in so-called "second-tier" and even "third-tier" cities is yet another factor feeding the growth of regional events. For example, whereas Baton Rouge, Louisiana, was a day trip for New Orleans conventioneers in the past, the addition of new conference facilities and hotels has now transformed it into a major competitor and attractive alternative to its more famous neighbor, New Orleans, to the south. The advantages of lower costs and new experiences are assets the creative event marketer can use effectively to draw attendance.

Duration of Stay

People have more to do, and less time in which to do it. Many events suffer the loss of attendance on the last day, as attendees get an early start back to the office, the factory floor, or home. There is nothing more deflating than to see a half-full room during the final session or closing banquet of your event because of early departures.

Promoters should coordinate with planners to ensure that the closing of an event is equal to the grand opening. There is an old saying related to the theater industry: "Have a great opening and a fabulous close, and the middle will take care of itself." While not literally true, the principle is that if attendees understand through marketing that they are going to see a slam-bang opening and a knock-your-socks-off close, they will arrive on time and stay through the final curtain.

In your marketing and promotion, stress the benefits of staying until the end with closing event features. Some examples of these features are listed in Figure 2-1.

Marketers should take a proactive role in creating the special features that will fulfill the mission of the event from beginning to end. Let your imagination be unrestrained and lobby your event sponsor to try those things that will attract interest, loyalty, excitement, and increased attendance.

- Honors and awards
- Door prizes
- Raffles
- Video highlights of the event, with interviews and candid pictures
- Drawings for free registration at the next event
- Silent auction
- Announcement of major organizational strategies or changes
- Special "Olympic" competition
- "Childhood pictures" contest (guess the identity of organizational leaders from blow-ups of childhood photos)

Figure 2-1
One of the greatest marketing challenges is that of holding the audience until the end of the meeting. Exciting awards, prizes, competitions, and postevent tours are often used to encourage this.

Car Keys to Success

One association, in order to protect its exhibitors from decreased attendance on the last day of the show, negotiated a partnership-marketing arrangement with an auto dealer to give away a new car to a lucky attendee during the final hour. The auto dealer was prominently mentioned in all advance publicity, and its general manager participated in the awards presentation.

Attendees stayed in large numbers to deposit cards for the raffle during the final day of the exhibits, and they gathered in a huge crowd to witness the drawing as the new car provided the backdrop for the event.

What was the key to holding the audience?

The winner had to be present to collect the new car keys at the drawing. Exhibitors and buyers stayed on to watch the festivities and congratulate the winner, and the trade press was on hand to interview and photograph the winner. In other words, rather than tailing off to an unexciting ending, the conference ended on the most exciting note of the three days of activities.

And from advance publicity to postconference press coverage, this promotional feature created an awareness of the event that compelled the sponsor to give away *two* cars the following year.

The Five Ws of Marketing

In facing the new challenges of marketing events, a continuous analysis of fact-finding must precede each campaign. This analysis must include the five Ws of marketing (see Figure 2-2). Dr. Joe Goldblatt, in *Special Events, Twenty-First Century Global Event Management,* states that the 5 Ws help determine if the event is feasible, viable, and sustainable. In event marketing, we use the same questions to determine the feasibility, viability, and sustainability of the marketing plan.

1. WHY?

When you look at promotional materials for events, the most glaring omission is often this essential element for encouraging attendance. You will probably see the name of the event, the organization's logo, the dates, and the location. That should be standard procedure.

We have already discussed the high demands on time and interest of potential attendees. A message simply stating that "You're Invited" or "Hope to See You" is passive and noncompelling to those who are inundated with print and electronic promotions. The event marketer must grab the target audience by the lapels and convince them that there are benefits that set your event outside the routine and drive those benefits into their most vital personal and professional interests.

The opening message of virtually all promotional materials should feature the "why?" Why should someone take the time and spend the money to come to your event? To answer that question, the marketing and management team for the event must determine the overriding reasons for the event itself.

When defined, those reasons must be addressed in hard-hitting and in *second-person terms* to those being sold on the idea of

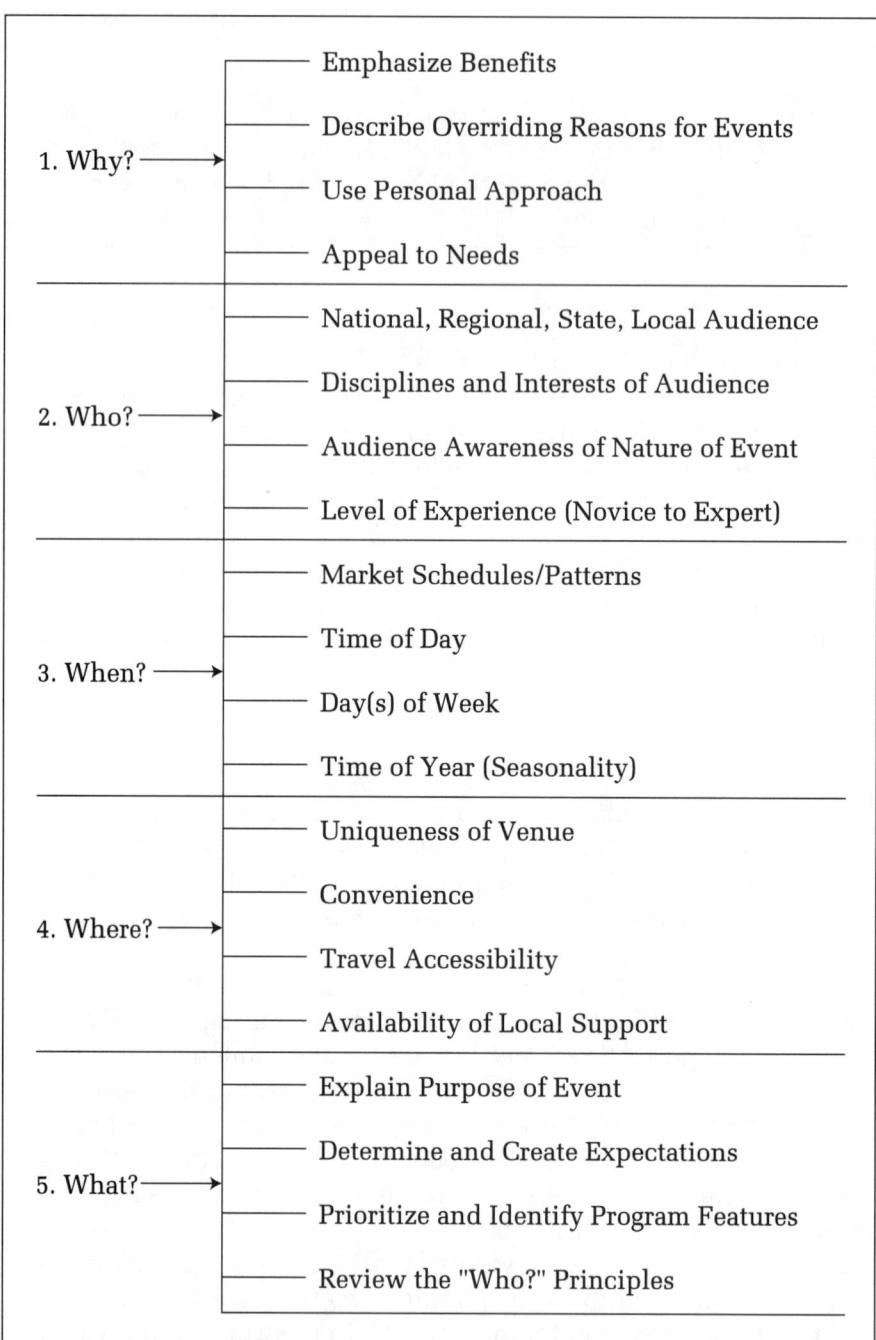

1. Why? →
    - Emphasize Benefits
    - Describe Overriding Reasons for Events
    - Use Personal Approach
    - Appeal to Needs

2. Who? →
    - National, Regional, State, Local Audience
    - Disciplines and Interests of Audience
    - Audience Awareness of Nature of Event
    - Level of Experience (Novice to Expert)

3. When? →
    - Market Schedules/Patterns
    - Time of Day
    - Day(s) of Week
    - Time of Year (Seasonality)

4. Where? →
    - Uniqueness of Venue
    - Convenience
    - Travel Accessibility
    - Availability of Local Support

5. What? →
    - Explain Purpose of Event
    - Determine and Create Expectations
    - Prioritize and Identify Program Features
    - Review the "Who?" Principles

Figure 2-2
The five Ws of marketing are critical to developing all promotional strategies. They must form the basis of all market research and development of the marketing message.

attending. Instead of the mundane call to attend your event with a simple "You're Invited"—*tell them why!* For example:

> You Will Learn How Your Business Can Survive and Grow in the 21st Century.
> The 38th Annual Convention: Be Where the Elite Meet.
> Be a Part of Our Industry's Revolution—or Be Left Out.
> The Race Is On. . .Learn How to Finish First.

The International Association of Convention and Visitors Bureau's "Destinations Showcase" is a one-day educational and exposition program, and its promotional brochure provides examples of "why" its target audience must attend. The message highlighting its 2001 conference is immediate, urgent, and compelling in listing the benefits for the attendees. These short, but arresting concepts are highlighted on the cover of the promotional brochure (see Figure 2-3). All of this is emphasized on the cover of the brochure, together with the date, location of the event, and preregistration deadlines. In other words, the five Ws are clearly described before the reader even opens the brochure.

In determining any marketing approach, whether it is an advertisement, a promotional video, a brochure, or a flyer, the process must begin with an analysis of the audience, the product, and the intrinsic assets of the event or the product that we want to promote.

With Figure 2-2 providing a broad overview, let us look at these elements in order.

2. WHO?

To whom are we marketing the event? Your target audience may vary, depending on the nature of the product being promoted. For example, a *national convention* may be aimed at the entire membership, past and potential exhibitors, past and potential sponsors, and related organizations.

A *training program* may be aimed primarily at those individuals whose disciplines and interests fall within the narrowly defined scope of the educational program being offered. The target marketing would avoid those whose educational needs are not consistent with the purpose of the program. A *product introduction* may be aimed at sales executives of a corporation, franchisees,

Figure 2-3
This brochure cover clearly addresses the five Ws of marketing.
It also attracts attention by listing compelling benefits of
attendance provided to fill the universal needs of most
consumers. *(Courtesy: International Association of Convention
and Visitor Bureaus)*

as well as trade publications, electronic media representatives,
and the consumer press.

A vigilant analysis of the audience to be attracted is essential
to target marketing, economy of printing, postage, list maintenance, and staff time.

3. WHEN?

Timing is everything! The enlightened management team should
make the marketing function an integral part of the planning
process in order to maximize the value of timing of an event.

Strategies in planning the timing of an event are integral to the challenges faced in the marketing process. And timing should also be carefully weighed in light of the schedules, patterns, and needs of the market being served. Scheduling conflicts with attendees present natural impediments to attendance. What are the elements that must be considered by the marketer?

Time of Day

A reception, for example, used to be planned for the end of the workday (such as 5:30 to 8:00 P.M.), allowing time for guests to finish work and gather prior to a dinner or departure for home. Increasingly, however, receptions are planned for mid-afternoon until early evening (e.g., 3:30 to 6:00 P.M.), giving guests the option of (and excuse for) leaving the workplace a bit early, spending an hour or two at the event, and then leaving early enough for their evening plans.

Days of Week

You should consider the days selected for the event carefully, factoring in the demographics of your market. A business event attracting CEOs and others in positions of authority might be much more attractive to the audience on a weekday than on a weekend, because they likely have the flexibility of attending on a workday and may be less willing to give up precious personal weekend time for a nonmandatory, business-related activity.

On the other hand, if you are marketing a street fair or carnival aimed at families, weekends are normally favored. Depending on the time of year, during weekdays the children may be in school (or summer school, which is becoming increasingly prevalent) and the parents will likely be at work. Therefore, weekends are more likely the most marketable option for family activities. Again, carefully consider the demographics and schedules of your audience in all your deliberations.

Time of Year (Seasonality)

When dealing with specific industries or professional constituencies, the time of year during which the target market is most available may be subtle, but critical. For example, in the hospitality and travel industry, most conventions are planned for mid- to late winter. Why? Because the potential attendees' most crucial times on the job are when they are serving other groups in their facilities and on their transportation systems.

Spring, summer, and particularly fall are the busiest times for transportation companies, hotels, and resorts, which are taking care of good-weather conventions, vacationers, and business meetings. Because their commerce and other business commitments are usually lighter in winter months, the potential attendees are more likely to be able to afford the time to attend your event. A careful analysis of the patterns of industry is essential to scheduling, which will have an enormous impact on marketing.

Local, Ethnic, and Religious Holidays

When marketing an event in a location with which you are not totally familiar, consider the potential conflicts (or opportunities) presented by local holidays. National holidays, such as the Fourth of July, Christmas, and Veterans Day, present many opportunities for event marketers to promote the celebration of that holiday during the event. These are the times replete with activities themed around the holiday festivities.

However, local holidays, which are not the reason for which the event is being held, may negatively impact the success of the

Pretty House—No One Home!

In a former life, I once marketed a study-mission and tour in Paris, France. My marketing thrust was affordability—and fun. The time of year was August. I was not aware that this time of year was the "holiday season" in Paris, and many of the shops, restaurants, and other Parisian features and attractions were closed because the city empties out as everyone celebrates the summer elsewhere. Month-long vacations are commonplace in Europe.

I soon discovered why the prices for accommodations and food functions were so affordable for my budget. There was little demand. It was a buyers' market for my group, a very affordable exercise. But it was greeted with a dearth of things to do, places to go, and personnel available to service our people.

event by interfering with the expectations of the attendees. Besides local holidays, marketers must be sensitive to ethnic and religious holidays and celebrations.

Whenever marketing an event outside of your normal venue, contact the convention bureau or chamber of commerce to determine local holidays or special events, such as parades or sporting events, and their effect on the daily pace and commerce of the city. You may find that the celebration can become an unexpected asset for your event—or, as in my case in Paris, a liability.

4. WHERE?

Location can be a key asset in promoting an event. A banquet event in a downtown arena may be emphasized because of the availability of public transportation or valet parking. Promotion for a golf outing at a prestigious country club may well emphasize as the "opportunity of a lifetime" playing the course, with the fundraising purpose of the event an added advantage to participating. A company meeting held on Navy Pier in Chicago rather than a hotel or convention center was positioned by an event planner as a unique opportunity to enjoy an event "on Lake Michigan," 3,000 feet offshore with a spectacular view of the Chicago skyline.

In other words, the location of the event can be a critical element in driving sales. Among the assets you should look for as benefits to promote are:

- In urban areas, the availability of public transportation, valet parking, convenience, and efficiency of travel
- In rural areas, a chance to enjoy panoramic views and pastoral scenery
- In shopping malls, an opportunity for centralized activities, ease of parking, and ancillary shopping and entertainment features to enjoy
- At resorts, the ambiance of pools, golf, upscale shopping, beaches, and gourmet dining
- At airport hotels, the inherent efficiency of getting the work done with minimum travel and commuting time because of the fly-in, fly-out design of the location

For bed-and-breakfasts, marketing materials can create a rustic environment of times gone by, augmented by a fire in the fireplace, home cooking, and perhaps even a ghost story or two. It is incumbent upon the marketing executive to look for the *unique* features of the location, capture these assets, and capitalize on them in attracting those guests who might not otherwise be compelled to attend for the program itself. Use the local convention bureau, chamber of commerce, and host facility to gain key promotional phrases and to learn all about the unique assets of the site. They know the features of the location and may even provide ancillary literature and photos to integrate into your marketing elements.

5. WHAT?

Every event is unique unto itself, or at least the marketing executives should present it as such. It may offer an opportunity to discover a new concept, a look into the future of the industry or trade, or a chance to view an innovative line of products and ideas. Regardless of the content you have identified, every event should be presented as refreshing and exciting.

Education and Training	Attendees will learn how to face tomorrow's issues.
Networking	Attendees will meet new friends and establish profitable business alliances.
Entertainment	Attendees will be mesmerized by the magic of our closing banquet.
"Choose Your Topic" Roundtable Sessions	Attendees will pick a topic and discuss it over coffee with colleagues.
"Support Your Charter School System"	Attendees will have an opportunity at our awards dinner to financially support our efforts for improved educational options for elementary school students in our community.

Figure 2-4

Most events provide a combination of the benefits listed here, as well as others more specific to the sponsoring organization. For marketers, the *purposes* of the event should be interpreted to illustrate the *benefits* awaiting the attendee.

In planning your promotion of any event, consider the *purpose* of the event. It may include any one—or any combinations—of these and others. Your first question should be "Why are we holding this event?" This is a deceptively simple, but also a critically essential question. For example, some of the benefits offered by the event, and the expectations of your attendees, are listed in Figure 2-3.

Regardless of the message or messages, the marketing mix must relate the benefits that will meet the expectations of the audience being pursued. Bear this in mind as you consider the "who" among the five Ws.

> *It's more important to reach the people that count . . . than to count the people you reach.*

Never Forget the Five Ws

Regardless of the nature of your promotion, whether it includes advertising, press releases, speeches, stunts, or brochures, the critical elements of "why, who, when, where, and what" must be emphasized *up front*—in the first paragraph of your press release, on the cover of the brochure, or in whatever medium of promotion you are using. It is the first axiom of journalism and promotion.

PROMOTION

A multifaceted approach to marketing, promotion could be defined as the stirring up of interest in your enterprise. The promotional campaign may include a wide range of marketing tools, or as few as one, depending on your products and your needs. Promotional techniques for event marketing may include advertising, public relations, cross-promotions (partnership marketing), street promotions, stunts, and public service "cause-related" events, among others.

You may find a promotional campaign for a national association convention or corporate meeting, for example, to include brochures, prepared speeches for chapter presidents and franchise leaders to deliver to home audiences, direct mailings, offers of prizes and vacation trips, and telemarketing efforts. On the other hand, a promotion for a local fundraiser may be limited to personal phone calls to potential benefactors and community leaders, enlisting their support for the event.

We have already discussed the circus parades staged by P. T. Barnum, which certainly increased public awareness that the circus was in town. But the promotional effort was much more than the parade itself; it also included the posters, press releases, advertising, requests for press coverage, press kits, and advance publicists that called attention to the entire enterprise.

There are many tools to be considered for use in a promotional campaign, among them:

- Letters
- Flyers ("single sheets")
- Brochures
- Mailing inserts
- Advertising
- Posters
- Speeches
- Postcards
- Street demonstrations
- Radio and television commercials in host venue
- Public service announcements
- E-mail, list serves, and e-commerce
- Tent cards at host facility
- Bus and subway signage (inside and outside)
- Press kits

These and other types of promotions should be selected on the basis of how you define your market or event. In addition, the amount budgeted to fund the effort will assist you in making that decision. We will discuss budgeting in Chapter 4. Because the full range of promotional tools can be enticing to marketing executives, it is essential to conduct market research to determine which of these tools will be most cost effective and generate the greatest return on investment.

ADVERTISING

One of the most predominant and traditional event promotion techniques is advertising. While most think of advertising in print form, involving newspapers or magazines, it may come in many forms that we see every day. Advances in electronic and broadcast technologies provide a platform for advertising on television and radio, over the Internet through "banner" ads and other inserts, and even on the big screen in movie theaters.

Marketers must be circumspect in selecting advertising media, because some may be controversial. Billboards are considered an intrusion on the environment by many, as are promotional posters attached to power poles, lining community streets, or stuffed into mailboxes.

Even Internet advertising has come under severe scrutiny. Its greatest weakness may be what was initially proclaimed as its greatest strength: the ability to precisely track the number of viewers and those who were interested enough to buy the product. For many, this was cutting-edge technology and an exciting approach to marketing products and services.

But, in many cases, Web surfers did not respond as predicted (they were more casual in their surfing habits than advertisers anticipated as they eagerly used the new electronic frontier). Even online companies themselves, which were expected to advertise their services on the Internet, have become much more selective in their advertising media selections. The result has been the failure of hundreds of dot-com enterprises whose advertisers could *quickly and precisely* conduct their own evaluations and research, enabling them to analyze the exact number of "hits" they were receiving or, even more critical to the equation, *not* receiving for their investment. The dollar volume of sales resulting directly from Internet advertising vis à vis the expenditures to advertise became an easy comparison to track.

Print advertising pervades our daily lives. As we have observed in the previous section, the images of event advertising come to us on the sides of buses, in our newspapers and magazines, on posters stapled to telephone poles, and on roadside signs, ranging from small neighborhood notices about a yard sale to huge billboards along our highways.

Association membership directories are often financed through advertising, as are community news organs, school yearbooks, association meeting brochures, and even church and synagogue bulletins. Event marketers should analyze the audience of any publication in order to determine the potential effectiveness of that investment. The Institute of Food Technologists (IFT) realized substantial gains by creating new advertising opportunities for exhibitors and other supporters. Its program book was 400 pages long, which constituted a huge expense item in the budget. In a short period of time, IFT was able to recover the cost of the program book and generate a 40 percent profit through the sale of ads to exhibitors, sponsors, and supporting organizations.

How do you decide on the right advertising instrument for your event needs? First, identify the audience you wish to attract. Then investigate the demographics reached by the advertising media you wish to consider. For example, marketing executives for larger events may consider broadcast media, which may reach a regional or even a national or international audience. More localized events will likely be promoted through community newspapers, local flyers or brochures, posters, and co-promotion with supporting groups and facilities. The primary consideration is the reach, or total impressions, of the group being sought, even before considering the demographic audience of the media being utilized.

Media sales representatives are equipped to demonstrate the demographics of their readers, listeners, and viewers. You should ask if the demographic data have been verified by an independent auditing firm. Ask when that audit was performed, and investigate the following criteria, among others of particular interest to you:

- Age
- Income range
- Trade or profession
- Gender
- Geographic location
- Race
- Marital status and family size

Psychographic Data

Event marketers should also analyze the psychographic profiles of their audience, namely, the values, attitudes, and lifestyles of the target market. An effective method for determining attitudes is through an attitude survey. This instrument will ask respondents to indicate preferences for a range of issues, from personal interests to educational needs to locations and timing of events. Attitude surveys may be conducted with quantitative or qualitative strategies or a combination of both. The purpose of the attitude survey is to gain an open and objective insight into the feelings of past, present, and potential attendees. You will want to construct the questions to address only those issues that are pertinent to your marketing efforts, inasmuch as the length of the survey will impact the number of responses (the longer the survey instrument, the fewer responses you may expect to receive).

A typical attitude survey will include questions such as the following:

- Have you attended our event in the past? Please check the years (list years).
- How many miles did you travel to attend?
- How would you rate the event? (Indicate Excellent, Good, Fair, Poor, or a numerical scale for rating.)
- Are you a member of the association?
- Did you register in advance or on site?
- Do you feel the registration fee is commensurate with the value of the event?
- Did you attend as a single participant, or with spouse, friend, or family? If not with family, why not?
- Please list the five educational programs you felt were most valuable. (List sessions by name, with check boxes.)
- Are the spring dates convenient for you? If not, please indicate which month fits your schedule best.

Obviously, the questions are as open ended as your need to know for the particular event you are marketing. Bear in mind, however, that while many commercially oriented surveys are off-putting to many, opinion and attitude surveys are more warmly received. People often enjoy having their opinions queried, and heard. You may not like the answers, but you can be assured they will guide a much more effective marketing campaign in the future.

Specialty Advertising

Creative marketers will find that advertising is not limited to magazines, newsletters, and brochures, but rather to virtually any item that will accept print.

We all have seen coffee mugs, refrigerator magnets, calendars, and note pads with advertising messages that the user sees daily.

We even buy (often at inflated prices) shirts, caps, and other apparel bearing the logos and slogans of the manufacturer or a sports team. We pay for the privilege of becoming walking billboards!

At your event itself, many opportunities exist for the marketing of the event and its sponsoring organization, creating not just a helpful item but also a memento of the event for the attendee to enjoy far beyond the final gavel. Tote bags may be imprinted with the name of the event and the sponsoring advertiser. This is an effective cross-promotion, which is often granted not just for an advertising fee but also to cover the cost of producing the bags themselves.

Directional and identification signs may carry the logo and name of the sign sponsor. Key rings, golf balls, alarm clocks, badge stickers, playing cards, and specially designed chocolate bars—the vehicles of specialty advertising—are limited only by the imagination. Many specialty advertising production companies exist with catalogs of preproduced advertising products designed to be imprinted with your logo, organization name, and a short message or slogan. The per unit cost of these imprinted specialty items will decrease as the quantity of your order increases.

Advertising approaches should be tested in advance for effectiveness. Many professionals use a "split approach," mailing a limited amount of advertising pieces featuring different colors, design, and paper weight to two control groups and then evaluating the response. Focus groups are also an effective way to judge messages, design, and positive acceptance.

Public Relations

Unlike advertising, which is primarily what you *say* about your organization or event in order to win acceptance, public relations is the promotional discipline of forming what your audience *thinks or feels* about the value of your enterprise and, even more important, about your organization as a whole. It is a broader, more time-consuming approach to building continuing allegiance to your cause and participation in your events. The goals of a public relations campaign may vary significantly, ranging from creating awareness of your event in its early stages of development, to continuing such awareness over a period of time, to offsetting negative publicity or controversies about the company or association that sponsors your event. Regardless, there are certain principles of public relations that will be employed.

The first step should be to examine previous public relations efforts and their relative effectiveness in promoting greater participation or in mitigating challenges. Were the responses positive or negative? Attitude surveys, focus groups, and analysis of attendance trends are helpful in this examination.

Public relations has become much more of a sophisticated marketing tool than the old days, when press agents tried to grab the lapels of newspaper reporters and gain a few column inches of coverage. Today, public relations professionals consider virtually all communications outlets in order to disseminate the message. Newspapers remain a staple outlet, as do radio and television broadcasters, magazines, newsletters, the Internet, and other online services. Related associations and corporations must also be considered as public relations resources, especially for their support of the event and their understanding of its purpose and their potential roles and mutual benefits. One of the greatest rewards of a positive public relations campaign is the discovery of partner marketers who will support your efforts in return for your support of theirs.

Scott Ward is vice president of the Widmeyer-Baker Group, a major marketing and communications company. Figure 2-5 lists his six steps to a successful public relations campaign.

The greatest asset of effective public relations is that it presents to your public *what others say about you* rather than what you say about yourself. In other words, an effective press release, personal approach, or media kit may result in editorial coverage in a newspaper. The value of an independently written article implies to the reader the *credibility* that may not be inferred from a paid advertisement. The Public Relations Society of America (PRSA), a professional society of public relations executives, estimates that the real value of editorial coverage is triple that of paid advertising. The impact can be illustrated in simple terms, according to PRSA, based on an average advertisement in a major U.S. newspaper:

½ page advertisement: Cost: $5,000
Editorial coverage of your event   Value: $15,000
in same space as advertisement

1. *Always Ask!* Do I need media? If so, why? Media coverage is a *means,* not an end. Stay focused on your overall goal.
2. *Define Your Goals.* What *specifically* are you trying to achieve?
3. *Target Your Audience.* Are you trying to attract students? Lawyers? Bricklayers? Men? Women? Cat owners?
4. *Select Your Media.* Focus on the media that will best reach your defined target market.
5. *Define Your Message.* Stay focused on message throughout the campaign. Be crisp, clear, and consistent.
6. *Find Your News Angle.* Look for the unique and unusual news about your event. Look for the *story* that will define your message. Ask yourself two key questions: What's the story here? And *why do we care?*

Figure 2-5
Public relations requires careful analysis of the project's purposes, audience, benefits, and the media available to deliver the appropriate message.

Press Materials

There are a number of tools available for the public relations effort: Press releases, press kits, media alerts ("requests for coverage"), organizational and event "fact sheets," specialty advertising items, flyers (also called "single sheets"), photos, and brochures.

Press Releases   Every press release should be designed according to the following format and with all the information outlined and in this order:

- Organizational letterhead or news release form.
- Name, address, phone number, fax number, and e-mail address.
- *Flush left:* A date for release to the public, or
- The boldfaced phrase "FOR IMMEDIATE RELEASE."
- *Flush right:* (For More Information: name of contact person and phone number).
- *Short headline* in bold capital letters.
- *Leading* the first paragraph, begin with release date and location (city) of release. The first paragraph should clearly de-

fine the five Ws of the event, with additional background and information in subsequent paragraphs.

- Information should be double-spaced (so editors may make notes) and printed on one side only.
- If the release is more than one page, signify by writing –*MORE*– at the bottom of the page. Begin the next page with the page number and the identification of the event or organization and continue with each succeeding page.

Alert the reader that the release is concluded by writing "End" or "# # #" at the close of the last page.

Content of the release should lead with the most important information, with additional details offered in a descending order of importance (see Figure 2.6).

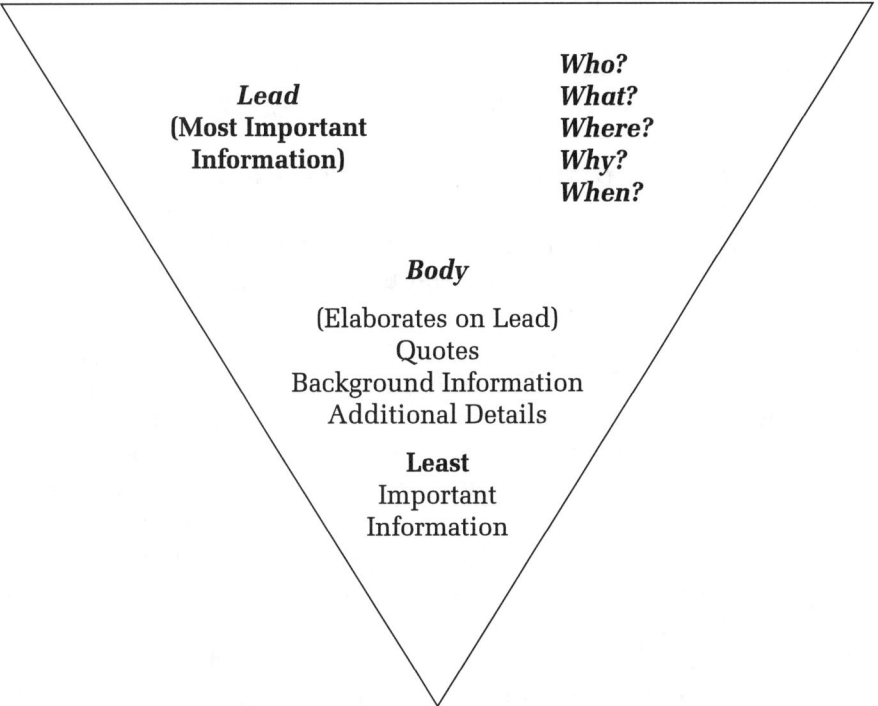

Figure 2-6
This "inverted pyramid" of the media release illustrates the need to begin with the most vital information (the five Ws) to capture the eye of the reader and encourage further review. *(Courtesy: The Widmeyer-Baker Group)*

Press Kits   A press kit is a more comprehensive tool used to relay as much information about an event and its purpose as possible, packaged in an attractive folder or portfolio imprinted with the name of the sponsoring organization, the event, a logo, and other pertinent information. Typically, press kits may contain:

- Press releases
- Photos
- Media alerts
- Requests for coverage
- Press conference announcements and invitations
- Speeches
- Background news stories
- Videotapes
- CDs or DVDs
- Organizational information
- Biographies
- Folders, brochures, postcards
- Advertising specialty items

Internal and External Event Public Relations

Smaller, individualized promotions such as advertising, remote broadcasts, stunts, and gift or prize giveaways are becoming an increasingly popular technique to be used for bringing attention to a more generalized product, service, or event. Our earlier example of a parade to call attention to the circus coming to town, together with coordinated advertising and posters, is a technique for using a specific celebration to call attention to a larger event.

Here is a more recent example. A local "oldies but goodies" radio station, WBIG, arranged with a major shopping center to have a Valentine's Day celebration in the mall to be broadcast live. The features would be a remote broadcast center, amplifiers, a stage, and a disc jockey to attract the crowd. The key draw was the hiring of a calligrapher (a hand-lettering artist) who had designed several original Valentine's cards and who would be on stage to hand-letter special inscriptions for all of those wanting a special (and free) handcrafted Valentine's message to take home to loved ones.

The station promoted the event liberally over its airwaves and advertised in local papers. At the event, the music, the awarding of prizes through a roulette game relating to music, and the personalized work of the calligrapher drew huge crowds to the mall, which translated into additional listeners for, and awareness of, the station. Internal and external public relations is often a blend of seemingly unrelated disciplines and interests to create a common bond. In this case, the marketing directors of both the station and the mall were integral to coordinating the success of the event.

This example also illustrates the value of cross-promotion, in this case the radio station, the shopping mall, the stores in the mall (which placed announcements in their windows, calling attention to the feature event), and the calligrapher herself. Additional traffic—additional sales.

Summary

The foundation for communications is built upon the five Ws. "Why, Who, When, Where, and What" must form the apex (and the lead paragraph or cover) of every press release, brochure, news story, request for coverage, e-mail promotion, and all other forms of marketing messages. The reader will be lost early on when those essential and compelling details are buried in the message. You have also been presented with a list of 15 promotional tools routinely used in marketing campaigns. Your challenge should be to come up with another 15, because the tools available are limited only by the imagination. Discretion must be practiced, however, to ensure that the tools selected are consistent with the values of your target markets.

Still another important point covered is that of the value of public relations as a marketing vehicle. An effective public relations campaign will impact what others say about your organization or client, rather than what you say about yourself. Credibility, or the lack of it, will be defined by the effectiveness of continuous attention to public relations as a long-term image builder for your organization. Sporadic public relations efforts, employed only when a company needs it to "pitch" a cause, could be seen as transparent and may well be damaging to the organization's image.

TALES FROM THE FRONT

A small city-center park named Franklin Square was derelict, crime-ridden, and a business-depressing eyesore for surrounding enterprises. A loose coalition of local business and association leaders formed, the purpose of which was to rehabilitate the park and turn it back over to the shoppers and office workers who avoided it each midday on their way to lunch or shopping.

The Franklin Square Association met once a month and developed internal/external public relations strategies. They began an annual Franklin Square Day, during which citizens would volunteer to clean up the park. Local television and radio stations were alerted through press kits and requests for coverage. The police department was enlisted for security. Local merchants were encouraged to provide food and soft drinks for the workers. The department of public works agreed to bring trucks and tools for raking, painting, and repair of long-abandoned fountains.

The result? Businesspeople and civic leaders showed up in work clothes to grab a rake and a paintbrush. Television and radio stations covered the event on both the 5 P.M. and the 11:00 P.M. news, with action coverage and interviews. Attention was called to the plight of the park and the people who were working to save it and the neighborhood. As a result, new supporters lined up to be included in the annual cleanup day.

Over the next 10 years, the number of volunteers grew and the park became a place for lunch, free concerts, and happy gatherings. It is now a showplace, with gleaming benches and a beautiful central fountain. Developers took note, and soon dilapidated buildings surrounding the square were replaced with new ones offering a multitude of shops, restaurants, and office space. The Franklin Square experience is an example of the power of public relations and the synergies it can bring to a community.

Chapter Challenge

Your city is planning to open its new town hall and courthouse in six months. A big celebration is being planned. You have been asked to market the event, for maximum exposure and citizen participation. You have been told that a press kit is necessary, but that you should seek other marketing avenues as well.

1. What items may you include in your press kit?
2. What details must you include in your press release?
3. What other community assets may you solicit to support the marketing program?

CHAPTER 3

Electronic Event Marketing Strategies

*The Danger in Communication Is the Illusion That
It Has Been Accomplished*

—*Voltaire*

**WHEN YOU HAVE COMPLETED THIS CHAPTER, YOU WILL
BE ABLE TO:**

- Develop an effective electronic marketing plan
- Identify the resources required to develop an e-marketing campaign
- Locate online event marketing registration providers
- Develop a complete e-marketing strategy
- Prepare copy for the Internet
- Promote your Web site
- Create banner ads
- Measure and evaluate your return on Internet event marketing

---

The *Computer Industry Almanac* states that over 350 million people are online today. That's over 5 percent of the world's adult population. And that number will only continue to grow. The Internet is quickly becoming known as the fourth medium of advertising, next to radio, broadcast, and print media. With its ease of use and initial low cost, marketers are quickly turning to the Internet as the wave of the future.

Note that although the online community is large, its reach is far less than TV, radio, and other advertising media. This means that although the Internet has a massive audience, it does not by any means reach the entire world. With this in mind, electronic marketing, in the beginning, should only be used as a *supplement* to any other promotion and/or advertising you do. Because this field is ever changing and growing, this chapter will cover broad generalizations and concepts of electronic marketing. It will not cover nitty-gritty details of "how-to" create a Web site or "how-to" design a banner ad, because as soon as it would go into print, those instructions would be obsolete.

The 14th annual *Communications Industry Forecast* stated that, by 2004, Americans will spend more hours annually, an average of 228, using the Internet than they will spend reading newspapers (147), books (92), and magazines (77). This means that as each year passes, more and more individuals will become Web savvy. Since the entire world population is not online, it may be helpful to know who is. The following "Internet user profile" was adapted from *Internet Marketing for Dummies:*

- The online world is still very American, which means online endeavors that are focused on Americans are more likely to get results.
- Other areas of the world, including Europe and Asia, are beginning to become more Internet savvy, so be ready in a few years to target these markets.
- English is the online language.
- Online users are financially well off, so use the Web to target the middle class or above.
- The majority of Internet users are between the ages of 25 and 44.

There are a variety of reasons that the Internet is the ideal marketing tool. It can reach millions of people, while also being used to target marketing at a smaller group of individuals. The 24 hours,

7 days a week availability is appealing. And there are no geographic boundaries.

Traditional marketing is often more expensive than online marketing, which makes using the Internet more cost effective. In addition, receiving instant results is very appealing. This not only allows immediate statistics, it also allows the marketer to review and adjust his or her campaign on a timely basis.

According to The George Washington University Event Management Certificate Program course, "Introduction to Event Information Systems," there are eight ways an event manager can utilize the Internet today. Jud Ashman, the professor of this course, refers to them as the eight Cs of electronic event systems.

1. **Communicate.** There is a large array of resources available for event managers to communicate on the Web. These include Web sites, e-mail, list serves, search engines, discussion groups, online ads, and Web site linking. All of these will be discussed throughout the book. Visit: **http://www.peoplelink.com.**

2. **Cut Costs.** The Internet offers a wide array of cost-saving methods for marketing. With no postage costs and lower phone bills, event managers can find themselves cutting costs for their event. Advertising dollars can also go farther by reaching more people on the Web.

3. **Conduct Research.** The Web is full of valuable resources and can provide the answer to almost any question. You can research venues, vendors, and target markets without even leaving your office. Visit: **http://www.cyberatlas.internet.com; http://www.demographics.com; http://www.factfinder.census.gov.**

4. **Commerce.** Not only can you shop for products for your event, but you can also sell items for your event, take registrations, and rent ads.

5. **Current Events.** You can keep abreast of trends and hot topics in your industry, as well as current events in your local area, nationally, and internationally. By using customizable Web sites and joining newsgroups, you can be updated on whatever topics or areas of interest you choose. Visit: C-Net News: **http://www.news.com; Wall Street Journal: http://www.wsj.com; http://www.entrypoint.com.**

6. **Command Attention.** By using Web resources to promote your event, you can call attention to your event. Web advertising can direct attention to your Web site. Direct e-mail

campaigns can hit your target market. Add your event to industry online calendars. Visit: **http://www.cvent.com; http://www.webadvantage.net.**

7. **Cutting-Edge Services.** Event management software can help manage the many tasks associated with planning a meeting. Online registration can help keep track of attendees and payments. Stakeholders from around the world can keep in touch by holding meetings online.

8. **Convenience.** Major aspects of event management can be accomplished right from your desk. You have access to information from around the world without even leaving your office.

Advantages of Web Marketing

Unlike traditional marketing, electronic marketing deals with "real time." Customers experience the most up-to-date information. By keeping your Web site up to date, you will keep customers coming back over and over again. *Net Results: Web Marketing That Works* lists the following advantages to Web marketing:

- **Brand Building.** Establishes an instantly recognizable brand by raising awareness of your site.
- **Direct Marketing.** Eliminates the costs associated with printing and mailing. The Web gives you the ability to constantly make appropriate changes to target your audience. Allows individualized messages to specialized audiences.
- **Online Sales.** Immediate order processing in an interactive environment.
- **Customer Support.** Easy access to frequently asked questions.
- **Marketing Research.** Provides valuable information about your customers. You can use demographics to tailor your site.
- **Content Publishing Services.** Makes information on your organization available to a wider Internet audience.

Developing an Electronic Marketing Strategy

When beginning to develop your electronic marketing strategy, John Fuhr, director of business development at Cvent.com, advises that event marketers take the traditional methods of marketing and find their online counterparts. In other words, use all the strategies you would during a direct-mail campaign and apply them to the Internet. For example, instead of sending a paper brochure, you would develop an online brochure.

BUSINESS PLAN

Before you can reap the benefits of online marketing, you must first know exactly what your business is all about. In addition to the standard business plan you have for your organization, you will also need a marketing plan. *The Unofficial Guide to Marketing Your Business Online* suggests doing one of the following to begin your online marketing plan:

1. Use a Web-based tool. Visit **http://www.bplans.com** to download and edit sample business plans.
2. Buy a business planning software. Palo Alto Software products **(http://www.paloaltosoftware.com)** offer easy-to-use packages, which will help you create a business plan.
3. Follow an online outline. Instead of creating your own, you may feel more comfortable following an existing plan. The Small Business Association (SBA) has a template for individuals to follow. Visit **http://www.sba.gov/starting/indexbusplans.html.**
4. Hire someone to write your plan. If writing your own plan is not your bailiwick, you can always hire someone else to do it for you. If you don't know someone, check out **http://www.guru.com,** which is an online forum that links independent contractors with projects.

DEFINE YOUR BUSINESS

Prior to marketing your event online, you need to clearly define your event and know your goals and target audience. It's important to perform the following:

- Determine clear and concise objectives and goals of the event.
- Establish the best way to position the event in the marketplace.
- Ascertain the strengths and weaknesses of the event.
- Identify the customer, to include demographics and consumer behavior.

- Define the competition.
- Differentiate this event from the competition.
- Evaluate the financial resources.
- Conduct comprehensive market research.
- Decide how best to reach the customer.
- Follow a detailed business plan.

RESEARCH

The Internet is one of the most valuable resources available for any kind of research, including market research. But do not get frustrated. With the abundance of information available, it sometimes can be a daunting task trying to find exactly what you need. The Internet can assist with finding:

- Market segmentation (what group is interested in your event?)
- Trends and demographics
- Competition evaluation
- Opportunities to identify new markets for your events

ESTABLISH THE ELECTRONIC MARKETING PLAN

There are a lot of options when deciding on what electronic methods to use for your marketing plans. A variety of these will be discussed throughout this chapter, including Web sites, online advertising, and e-mail campaigns.

WEB RESOURCES—THIRD PARTY PROVIDERS

Creating a presence online is an intimidating project. So why not turn to Web professionals for help? There are online companies that can help you make this an easier process. These companies can help you from beginning to end make the process of electronic marketing less overwhelming. By turning to a professional, you can have experts at your fingertips to help you pull together an impressive and cohesive campaign. Web site marketing is all driven by one important factor: What are your goals? These organizations can assist you in reaching those goals by helping to (1) create a clear vision, (2) implement a marketing plan, (3) execute the plan, and (4) evaluate the results. A good example of a company that can assist in this process is Web Ad.vantage, which can be reached at **http://www.webadvantage.net.**

If your marketing plan is already created and you just need some assistance in marketing the registration aspect, Cvent is an excellent company to turn to. Cvent is revolutionizing the meetings and events industry with its suite of powerful tools, which include online registration and e-marketing and data analysis tools. Cvent's product greatly improves attendance, efficiency, and cost effectiveness. And it is easy to set up. In a matter of minutes after completing the "Campaign Wizard," you have created a personalized targeted campaign. Cvent's Web-based software uses an organization's existing database to create and send targeted e-mail communications, which include invitations, reminders, confirmations, postevent follow-ups, and other promotional mailings.

While all of these added features make it easy for the customer or attendee to reply, they also make life easier for the planner. As with many online registration tools, planners have access to real-time statistics. No more waiting for an individual to enter the registration information into a database and then wait for the accounting department to approve payment. Everything is completed online and processed immediately.

Companies such as Cvent may offer a great return on your investment. They do this by:

- **Saving Money.** By reducing or eliminating design, printing, faxing, and direct-mail costs. With real-time attendance statistics at your fingertips, you can save money with more accurate head counts.
- **Increasing Attendance.** One-to-one marketing tools make exceeding attendance goals easy. With prepopulated online registration forms, your guests will appreciate the convenience you offer them.
- **Saving Time.** Increased staff productivity through automation of registration, payment, and marketing.
- **Increasing Response.** Instant response within minutes of launching a campaign. Through automated personalized reminder and confirmation e-mails, your campaign becomes more effective.
- **Providing Immediate Results.** Responses, reporting, and statistics on customers at your fingertips.
- **Improving Your Data.** Marketing efforts can only be as good as the information in your database. By using online surveys, you can capture customer needs and preferences, as well as their most up-to-date contact information.

Visit the Cvent site at **http://www.cvent.com** for more information. Other online resources offering similar tools are b-there.com **(http://www.b-there.com)** and Event411 **(http://www.event411.com).**

Doug Fox, publisher of the *EventWeb Newsletter,* says that "Tools that integrate email marketing and data analysis with online registration are the killer applications for the meeting industry today." Online registration was previously viewed as a customer service tool and a way for attendees to register quickly. The next stage of Web-based registration is thinking in marketing terms. Once you start integrating online registration with e-mail marketing, you have a very powerful offering that allows you to deliver personalized messages to prospective customers and encourages them to sign up for your meeting.

Marketing Your Event on the Internet

Kevin Dolan, e-business development manager of Microsoft Corporation, has taken the five Ps of traditional marketing (product, price, place, public relations, and positioning) a step farther for Web marketing. He recommends following these Ps to help establish a great Web marketing campaign:

- **Presence.** Having a placeholder on the Web is the first step. The main goal of your entire electronic marketing campaign will be to drive the traffic there.
- **Pleasing.** Make it pleasing to the eye.
- **Personalized.** Develop a relationship through personalization.
- **Purchase.** Through e-commerce, buy or sell products or services.
- **Process.** Integrate your Internet site with core business systems.
- **Partnership.** Being connected with partners, suppliers, customers, and competitors expands your reach.
- **Programmable.** The Web can be easily changed to tailor your marketing message.

EVENT WEB PAGE DEVELOPMENT

The development of an event Web site takes as much time, thought, and consideration as developing your overall marketing strategy. The design should ensure easy navigation and should be designed to serve your customers' needs. Jud Ashman recommends these key points when creating an event e-site:

- Structure
- Ease of navigation
- Style
- Technical requirements
- Consistency
- Personalization

Choosing your event domain name is very important. Web site addresses live and die by their ability to be recognized, according to *Net-Marketing: Your Guide to Profit and Success on the Net*. All domain names must be registered with Network Solutions Registration Services **(http://www.internic.net).** The registration process is simple and can be completed online. New domain names cost $100 for a two-year maintenance fee. After that, a $50 fee will be charged annually. The process takes a few weeks.

If at all possible, your domain name should incorporate some of the keywords in your event title so customers can easily find your site. Keywords are an important consideration when developing your site, because, when you register with search engines, they use the keywords section to find your site. One Web site, however, should only focus on a few keywords in order to get high rankings in the search engines. The search engines section describes this area in more detail.

According to *Meeting News,* Web surfers have a limited attention span. To grab their attention immediately, your opening page should clearly define the focus of your event, the intended audience, and the benefits of participation. *Meeting News* also lists other important considerations when designing a Web site:

- Your Web site does not need to be elaborate, but it must be attractive enough to motivate prospective attendees to read your marketing materials.
- Make it easy for attendees to stay in touch with you. Visitors of your site may not be ready to register immediately, but by providing your e-mail address, organization mailing address, other contact information, and a link to conference materials, they can quickly get in touch with you.
- Materials should be easy to print. Many people need to get

their boss's approval before attending. Some are more traditional and prefer to print them out and read them.
- Include an FAQ (frequently asked questions) section.

Having related links to other areas of interest to your audience is a valuable resource to provide. It impresses your customers and shows them that you are a leader in the marketplace. Creating reciprocal links with other sites can also bring more traffic to your site. Many businesses trade referrals with other businesses on the Web, just like they would offline. To negotiate this process, you would identify companies that might be interested in trading links with your site. According to Deborah Whitman of Microsoft Corporation, this can help you by creating more traffic, and it can also improve your ranking on search engines such as Google. She offers these six suggestions for identifying the types of businesses with which to create exchange relationships:

1. Companies that offer complementary products or services
2. Unrelated companies that serve your customers
3. Local businesses
4. Suppliers and distributors
5. Chambers of commerce and other community organizations
6. Competitors

Once your event Web site is developed, do not forget to include your Web URL (uniform resource locator) address on *everything* that is printed. This includes brochures, faxes, press releases, business cards, and advertisements.

Writing for the Internet is very different from writing for other marketing pieces. Web Ad.vantage has five important rules to follow when creating copy for a Web site:

1. **Speak to the "Everyperson."** When developing your Web site, aim to keep it simple so everyone can follow. Unlike traditional marketing pieces, conversational language is becoming more common, as well as unconventional writing such as slang and catch phrases. The key is to build a relationship with the individual.
2. **Keep It Tight.** Don't feed your readers too much information or you will lose them. Keep paragraphs short, use bullets, utilize larger font sizes, and insert graphics when possible.
3. **Get Feedback.** Have someone critique your site, preferably someone outside of your industry, and definitely not your

family, friends, co-workers, or subordinates. Take the criticism seriously and adjust your site as necessary.

4. **Remember the Web's Disjointed Nature.** The Web does not flow nicely from page to page like a book does. Since Web pages often have no relation to one another, it's crucial to repeat important information over and over on each page. Remember that users may enter your Web site from a page you did not intend them to use.

5. **Have Something Important to Say.** All information on your site should include substance.

For more information on writing for the Web, check out **http://www.thewritemarket.com.**

Ways to enhance your Web site:

- Include a "Make This Site Your Home Page" option.
- Create easy referral links where people can tell their co-workers, friends, and families about the site.
- Host a weekly "opt-in" newsletter.

The following Web sites keep customers coming back:

http://www.amazon.com
http://www.1800flowers.com
http://www.sears.com

When developing your event Web site, think about what makes you frustrated when surfing the Web. Some of these frustrations may include:

- Omitted information
- Slow-loading pages
- Difficult-to-find sites

You must eliminate these obstacles to promote use of your site.

PROMOTING YOUR SITE

Once the design phase is complete, you have to direct people to your site. *Meeting News* offers eight easy ways to encourage attendees to visit your site:

1. List the Web address for your event on high-traffic search engines and directories (e.g., Yahoo!, AltaVista, HotBot, and Excite).

2. Become listed on meeting and event calendars. Visit: **http://www.tscentral.com; http://www.tsnn.com; http://www. associationcentral.com.**

3. Consider exchanging links, sponsorships, or advertising with other Web sites.

4. Distribute news releases online. Visit: **http://www.business-wire.com; http://www.prnewswire.com; http://www.digital-work.com; http://www.prweb.com.**

5. Include your Web address everywhere you can (i.e., printed collateral, ads, etc.).

6. Identify e-mail discussion groups or lists related to your industry and become an active participant.

7. Use the signature file at the end of your e-mail to provide your contact information, as well as your event information. Make those few lines compelling.

8. Exchange links with exhibitors, so their customers can become informed about the event.

In addition to the above ideas, Web Ad.vantage offers these other low-cost ways to promote your site:

- Buy low-cost advertising on targeted e-mail newsletters.
- Develop your own opt-in e-mail list and send out notices, updates, special offers, and so on.
- Develop an affiliate program.
- Visit **http://www.recommend-it.com** for free referral information.
- Customize specialty advertising giveaway items with each sale or registration.
- Write a letter to the editor of a favorite magazine or journal for your target audience.
- Give something free away on your event Web site and then register with free-for-all sites such as **http://www.freecenter.com** or **http://www.free.com.**

INTERNET EVENT ADVERTISING

Online advertising is designed to yield instantaneous, easily measurable results. According to *Internet Marketing for Dummies,* the Internet is both the ideal medium and the worst medium for advertising. The good news is that a part of Internet ads are easily trackable by how many people "click through" the ad. A typical "click-through rate" on an Internet ad is less than 1 percent. Tracking advertising will be discussed later in this chapter.

Part of Internet event advertising is not captured but is future business caused by the ad. Those people who take future action after seeing an ad cannot be tracked. This is called "image" or "brand" advertising and just like in other media (newspaper, radio, TV) is much more difficult to track.

A decision that needs to be made is how you will advertise online. Will you use "house ads" by advertising on your own site? Will you promote your event on other sites? Will you allow others to advertise on your site?

Event Banner Ads

Banner advertisements involve space that is sold on someone else's Web site for use by another. A few years ago, banner ads were simple static ads placed across the top of a Web site. Now new technology allows interactive advertisements with animation, video, and sound clips. Although a few years ago, banner ads had over a 2 percent response rate, the response rate has dropped to as low as 0.5 percent as banner ads have become more prevalent.

Microsoft's Bcentral.com offers the following tips when using banner ads:

1. Keep it short and simple.
2. Make the benefits relevant.
3. Capture interest, pique curiosity.
4. Use promotions and contests.
5. Have a call to action to give people a reason to click.
6. Make the message fit the goal.

Ezines and Newsletters

Advertising in an ezine, or electronic newsletter, is one of the most recommended forms of Internet advertising. These forums are highly targeted, are relatively inexpensive, and typically have a higher return on investment than other ads. Because subscribers join or "opt in" to these newsletters, this is not considered a form of "spam," or unwanted communications. Michael Southon, publisher of the *Free Directory of Ezines,* offers the following 10 tips for successful ezine advertising:

1. **Track Your Ads.** This is even more important if you are placing multiple ads at the same time. The simplest way is to place a key code at the end of an e-mail or URL address. You can code an e-mail by following this format when establishing your e-mail address: yourname@yourdomain. com?subject=ezineA. Or you can use a free Web statistics program.
   Try: **http://www.hitbox.com**
          http://www.openwebscope.com

2. **Target Your Audience.** By using the "subject categories" in an ezine directory listing, you will be able to find an ezine that relates to your event audience.

3. **Subscribe to the Ezine First.** Once you have chosen a number of ezines that target your particular audience, subscribe to them first and examine their ads closely. If you see a repeating ad, you can guess that it's getting good results.

4. **How Many Ads Appear in Each Issue?** Check the ezine for the number of ads. If there is an abundance of ads, the response rate is probably not too great. Readers of these publications may have begun ignoring the ads.

5. **Are There Any Competing Ads?** Your ad will be much more effective if there is no competition in the issue.

6. **Small Ezine Versus Large Ezine?** Bigger is not always better. The larger publications often have more advertisers, which means you may not be as visible. And smaller ezines may be more targeted.

7. **Repeat!** Research shows that, off the Web, an ad has to be seen nine times before someone acts on it. Many ezines offer discount packages. If your budget is very small, try to advertise at least three times per publication.

8. **E-mail Address Versus URL?** By giving an e-mail address as opposed to a URL link, you are able to send a powerful, targeted response. It is also much easier to track an e-mail than a URL address.

9. **Offer Something Free.**

10. **Keep Your Ad Short.** Shorter ads are more likely to be read. Keep sentences short and use the word "you." Instead of describing the event, tell readers why they must attend.

Get more information on the "Free Directory of Ezines" at **http://www.netmastersolutions.com.**

Advertising Purchasing Options

Most online advertising is sold in two forms: cost per thousand impressions (CPM) and cost per click (CPC). A CPM is based on the number of times that the advertisement is shown online, while a CPC is based on the number of clicks produced by the advertisement. The CPC might seem like the obvious first choice, but be careful; unless it's placed on a well-trafficked Web site, it may not be a better option.

Don't forget to negotiate and ask for discounts when starting out. Many ezines offer new-campaign specials. This allows you to test certain markets before you make a large financial investment. Advertising reps should be willing to work with you, especially if you pledge your commitment to them, if the advertising campaign is successful.

When purchasing ad space, don't forget to ask these important questions, provided by Web Ad.vantage:

- What is the site's per month traffic? If the advertising rep does not answer this question or does not provide you statistics, be wary. You may be buying space on a weak site or paying too much for that space.
- What kind of ad click-through tracking statistics does the site provide?
- What is the monthly minimum?

Remember to learn from experience. Permit yourself to make some mistakes. Advertising purchasing is not an exact science. Do the best you can and keep trying.

SEARCH ENGINES

One of the most important ways to generate traffic to your event Web site is to get listed on all the popular search engines and directories. To understand the importance of this, review the results of a study completed by RealNames (**http://www.realnames.com**):

- Over 85 percent of Web users use search engines.
- 50 percent of Web users spend 70 percent or more of their time searching online.
- 70 percent of those surveyed know specifically what they are looking for when they use a search engine.
- 44 percent of Web users say they are frustrated with Web navigation and search engine use.

- 20 percent of Web users completely give up when unable to find what they are looking for; the rest will try another search engine.

To register your event, visit each of the search engine Web sites and follow their instructions closely. This will help ensure inclusion. For those who want to stay ahead of the market and on top of the search engine list, there is a way to be guaranteed to be among the leaders, by paying for your ranking. Google, GoTo, and AltaVista, to name a few, all offer this new option. Visit **http://www.google.com, http://www.goto.com,** and **http://www.altavista.com.** This means that when a user performs a search using specific search terms, the results will be shown in descending order according to the price paid per click. As the marketer, you would choose certain keywords or phrases that you would like to have ranked. Your bid would be for a price that you would pay each time someone clicks on your selection. Note that each site has very specific conditions to follow to be included in the bidding. So observe those carefully if you want your bid to be accepted. Also, as the number of search terms expands, so will the bid price, and your link could be bumped by a higher bid.

There are many who dislike this practice because it edges out the individuals with less money and hides the true search results. This can cause confusion to certain customers.

Some of the most popular search engines:

- About **(http://www.about.com)**
- AltaVista **(http://www.altavista.com)**
- AOL **(http://www.aol.com)**
- Ask Jeeves **(http://www.ask.com)**
- Excite **(http://www.excite.com)**
- Go.com **(http://www.go.com)**
- HotBot **(http://www.hotbot.com)**
- LookSmart **(http://www.looksmart.com)**
- Lycos **(http://www.lycos.com)**
- MSN **(http://www.msn.com)**
- WebCrawler **(http://www.webcrawler.com)**
- Yahoo! **(http://www.yahoo.com)**

KEYWORD BUYS

Purchasing of keywords can come in many forms, ranging from banner ads to paid-for listings. Search engines use these ads when the user searches for a particular term or keyword. For example, if you bought the keyword "balloon," everytime someone used the keyword balloon, your ad would pop up. Sites such as Yahoo! and AltaVista offer keyword buys.

Be aware that the more common the word, the more expensive the purchase may be. If you are very careful when choosing your keyword, this can provide very precise target marketing. When purchasing this option, it's a good idea to purchase it on a "click-through" basis versus "times viewed." This will ensure that you are paying for someone actually seeing your ad.

PERSONALIZING YOUR EVENT MESSAGE

The Internet has become the preeminent niche-marketing tool. As you begin to identify your event target audience, it becomes easier to focus your marketing efforts on specific groups in specific ways. "Cookies" can be used to remember your guests' names, as well as their Web-surfing habits. This tool provides a great customer service benefit to the guests visiting your site. For more information on cookies, visit **http://www.cookiecentral.com.**

E-COMMERCE FOR YOUR EVENT

To use your Web site as a profit center, encourage visitors to buy some sort of product or take some sort of financial action while visiting your site. If you do not have the information technology (IT) staff to manage this yourself, Web-hosting companies are available for outsourcing. These companies allow implementation of the "shopping-cart" service without any additional programming needs and sometimes for as little as a few hundred dollars. You can also set up a shopping service on sites such as **http://www.store.yahoo.com.** Monthly fees range from as little as $10 a month to over $100 a month, depending on the site and services chosen.

SPONSORSHIP/PARTNERSHIP

Not all visibility is gained through advertisements. Establishing partnerships or sponsorships with other organizations is a fabulous way to not only gain exposure but make money. This process can work in two ways. You can place your event on other Web sites, as well as opening your site up to others. This could involve the exchange of money (e.g., the selling of advertising space) or could involve a "trade-out" where no money is exchanged. When developing your strategic partners, you can promote one another through banners, buttons, text, links, and direct on-site sales. Partners can even develop co-branded pages where they promote each other together.

These are the five basic types of electronic sponsorship:

1. **Branded Content.** The advertiser does not play a role in creating or shaping the content; it is the publisher's responsibility.
2. **Event Promotions.** The advertiser plays a role in developing content in conjunction with the publisher.
3. **Advertorials.** This differs from traditional methods of print because there is more of a willingness to display material that is pleasing to the advertiser.
4. **Microsites.** This option expands the notion of the advertorial to multiple ad/content pages, similar to special pullout sections in magazines and newspapers.
5. **Portals.** This is perhaps the most confusing among sponsorship opportunities. In this option, one site agrees to merge its content with that of another site as a service to Web surfers, thus creating a brand value to the content provider.

AFFILIATE OR ASSOCIATE PROGRAMS

These programs are designed for the sole purpose of directing targeted traffic to an event site. These programs are one of the best online marketing tools available to small businesses because there is no financial risk. In a nutshell, affiliate marketing is simply revenue sharing between online merchants (someone selling a good, product, or service) and the affiliates (content sites). Affiliates are given links by the merchant to place on their site with the intent of receiving quality traffic and expecting a percentage related to a desired action (i.e., registration, sales, downloads, etc.).

With these programs, you only pay if a customer performs an activity on your site (i.e., registers for an event, makes a purchase, signs up for an e-mail list, or whatever product or service you want the customer to get). This differs greatly from advertising, where you pay the fee up front and hope it delivers. Affiliate marketing allows you to pay *only* after the results are delivered. With these programs, you agree to pay another business (your affiliate) a referral fee for each customer who completes an activity at your Web site.

For more information on affiliate marketing, investigate:

Commission Junction: **http://www.cj.com**
Be Free: **http://www.befree.com**
Performics: **http://www.performics.com**

Microsoft Bcentral.com offers five tips for making affiliate marketing live up to its potential for you:

1. Seek good offers that provide graduated levels of investment.
2. Offer a variety of links.
3. Find the right affiliates.
4. Actively recruit affiliates.
5. Take care of your affiliates once you have selected them.

There are a variety of programs; therefore, finding the right one, or creating your own, may be a challenge. After joining a program, be sure to continue to evaluate its performance and track its effectiveness. With a bit of effort, affiliate marketing can increase online activity by up to 15 percent. These programs do take time to administer, but they can be worth it. Amazon.com has over 450,000 affiliates sending it new customers. This could be you!

LINKING

Long before there were sophisticated marketing tools like banner ads, affiliate programs, and sponsorships, there was the simple hyperlink. By linking your site with others, you can generate more traffic to your site. Web Ad.vantage offers great tips on successful linking. Visit its "Marketing Tip Archive" at **http://www. webadvantage.net.**

DISCUSSION GROUP

Online discussion groups are a great way to market your business, services, and events, but do know that there are etiquette rules to follow. Web Ad.vantage offers three tips to help you avoid crossing that ethical boundary:

- **Understand Where You're Posting.** Don't just presume that you can plaster your event message all over the place once you join a group. That is the equivalent of discussion group spam. Instead, spend a little time belonging to the list before posting (this is called "lurking"). By doing this, you can learn the tone used by participants, what types of subject matter they discuss, and any possible sore spots.
- **Don't Sound Too Commercial.** Make certain your sales message is subtle.
- **Play Upon Your Expertise.** If at all possible, don't even mention your event affiliation. Consider answering a question with legitimate information that proves you are an expert in the field. Then be sure to sign your post with your name, affiliation, URL, and contact information.

ONLINE SURVEYS

Just as important as monitoring the Web site traffic and the number of visitors you have is knowing who your visitors are. If you know your Web site audience and their demographics, you can market your site more directly to the intended audience. One of the most efficient ways to do this is by conducting surveys. What questions you ask will be determined by what you want to know. Do try to keep surveys short and don't forget to ask a bit of background information, without getting too personal. The following survey services can help create, house, and distribute online surveys. The list is provided by Web Ad.vantage:

- **http://www.zoomerang.com.** Allows the easy creation of online surveys.
- **http://www.surveysite.com.** Specializes in independent Web site evaluations, online focus groups, pop-up surveys and polls, and e-mail surveys.
- **http://www.infopoll.com.** Offers online survey software, enabling anyone to create questionnaires and collect instant feedback.

- **http://www.add-a-form.com.** Offers free "public domain" survey forms as well as a professional series of custom-built, paid-for surveys.

E-COMMERCIALS

A TV-like advertising campaign has hit the e-marketing world. eCommercial.com has created a revolutionary tool, bringing audio and video commercials to the Internet. Its 30-second commercials are supplemented with hot links to various sites and its technology tracks customer hits. For more information on this innovative tool, visit **http://www.crn.com/ebiz.**

There are many other online ways to serve your organization or client. They may deal directly with marketing and are strategies you may want to consider to enhance your event. The *EventWeb Newsletter* suggests the following:

- Internet broadcasts and streaming video
- Virtual trade shows
- Online auctions
- Online education

E-MAIL

E-mail is not only efficient, it is also an effective way to communicate information. From a marketing position, e-mail allows the event marketer to test a variety of messages, create links to the organization's Web site, gather information electronically, and encourage faster and higher response rates while saving money.

15 Successful Steps to Event E-mail Networking

1. **Getting Started.** Join discussion lists, subscribe to newsletters and ezines, and participate in Usenet newsgroups. Offering assistance and expertise on a particular subject or asking for help will begin the "know, like, and trust you" part of the networking process.

2. **Introductions.** Determine the introduction policy of each forum and send out an introduction about you and your firm. Include information on who you are, what you do, and what kind of clients you are looking for.

3. **Signature Files.** With each request for help, answer to a question, introduction, or other e-mail correspondence, include a signature file where it is appropriate. I do participate on lists where no one uses a signature file, so make sure that you follow the list protocol when using signature files.

4. **Autoresponders.** By far, this is one of the most successful networking tools. An autoresponder automatically sends out information from a simple e-mail request sent to it. They can be used for so many things, including:
   - Promotional material
   - Product/service information
   - Hiring help
   - Training help
   - Article distribution

5. **Ads.** E-mail *cannot* be used to send ads to folks who have not requested the information. However, you can run ads in various e-mail forums, ezines, and newsletters. Be *very* sure to check forum protocol on this usage.

6. **Product Delivery.** There are many firms that can actually deliver their product via e-mail. Consultants, software companies, authors/writers, and trainers can transport their product and service via e-mail, reducing costs significantly.

7. **Follow-Up.** Timely updates, greetings, or, in some cases, general information can be distributed via e-mail. Follow-up is something done with existing clients or persons who have expressed an interest in future contact. It isn't follow-up if there has been no previous request for information.

8. **Customer Service.** Being able to reply quickly and efficiently to event guests' requests, questions, and complaints is an extremely valuable networking tool.

9. **Newsletters and Articles.** One of the most important tools available for establishing credibility is the use of articles you have personally written. Submission of those articles to targeted newsletters and ezines is quite effective. Once you have enough material, you can even start your own newsletter.

10. **Media Releases.** Many editors of both online and offline publications prefer to receive press releases via e-mail. As with all other forums, it is necessary to ascertain that the editor does indeed want releases via e-mail.

11. **Moderating/Guest Moderating.** Most really useful e-mail lists and newsgroups are moderated, meaning there is a person who is responsible for keeping the group on track, preventing the wrong type of messages from appearing on the list. You can start your own moderated group, or you can volunteer to "guest-moderate" a group you are comfortable handling.

12. **Contests.** You can use e-mail to announce, run, and promote a contest. Again, be sure to check the forum policy on contests before posting any kind of announcement to that forum.

13. **Research.** E-mail is a powerful research tool. It is very easy to send requests for information via e-mail.

14. **Organization.** E-mail can keep you organized and productive. Through the use of filters (mechanisms in your e-mail program that automatically sort your mail for you) and a set of masters (e-mail messages already written that you can send in response to frequently asked questions or commonly requested information), you will find that you can handle hundreds of e-mail transactions in just a few hours a day.

15. **Personal E-mail.** It is through your personal correspondence that you will intimately get to know people, and they you. It is not only possible to "read" people via e-mail (and therefore get to know, like, and trust them), but is almost impossible not to be able to do so, as long as you are aware of personality styles.

Source: Adapted from Nancy Roebke, **http://www.profnet.org**.

Events involve many avenues of communication between the planning organization and the attendee. Each time you communicate with your attendee, it is an opportunity to build a relationship and add value. *Association Meetings* magazine lists the top six messages that every event marketer should consider:

1. **Initial Invitation.** This is usually the first communication and will contain all the details, values, propositions, and marketing messages, encouraging the individual to register.
2. **Follow-Up Marketing.** This is similar to the initial invitation, but should contain a slightly different marketing message for those who did not respond the first time.
3. **Event Registration Confirmation.** This assures the attendee that his or her registration was received and processed correctly. For fee-based events, this message can serve as a payment receipt. It also provides an opportunity to confirm personal information, event information, and any special requests.
4. **Regret Message to Declines.** This message can add a touch of class and help forge stronger relationships by communicating in a positive way. This is also a great opportunity to let declines know how to obtain materials related to the event.
5. **Event Reminder.** This message, above all, can assist in building stronger relationships. The reminder should include basic logistical information, changes in programming, and any balances due for the event.
6. **Postevent Thank You.** Besides showing your appreciation, a thank-you message is an additional opportunity to sell merchandise, make educational material available, and allow for feedback.

E-mail marketing is a cost-effective method because it can cost as little as pennies per message. That's quite a bargain when compared to traditional direct mail, which can cost over a dollar per piece.

Tim Mack states in "Electronic Marketing: What You Can Expect" that e-mail marketers will follow the same "40-40-20" rule of direct-mail marketing. The rule states that the copy, graphics, and other "creative" elements only comprise 20 percent of the strength of the campaign. The rest of the campaign's strength is 40 percent offering the right price or product and 40 percent reaching the right audience.

BROADCASTS

If you do not have your own in-house list, using a third-party service is one of the most credible ways to send broadcast e-mails. Third-party services can provide a list of individuals who have chosen to receive information. This is referred to as "opt in." The e-mail should come from the third party so its address appears in the "sender" field and the e-mail is not perceived as "spam" or junk mail. Companies such as Web Ad.vantage **(http://www. webadvantage.net)** can help you strategically plan an e-mail campaign. If you have an established campaign, you can go directly to list brokers to purchase an e-mail list.

LIST SERVES AND MAIL LISTS

Always include an "opt-out" device in your message, whereby an individual can ask to be removed from a particular mailing list. On the flip side, there should always be an "opt-in" link, whereby an individual can receive more information about an event or product. Note there are etiquette rules to follow when replying to messages so please follow your particular list's rules.

PERSONALIZATION

E-mail event marketing campaigns offer many advantages over a traditional direct-mail campaign. John Fuhr, director of business development with Cvent, stresses one of the best benefits is the ability to target certain segments of your audience. For example, if you are trying to attract members, nonmembers, students, and exhibitors all to the same event, instead of sending them all the same brochure as you would in the mail, you can now tailor it to their specific needs. For each letter and attachment you send, you can highlight areas of interest that pertain directly to them. And don't forget—e-mail is low cost or even free! So you are saving a great deal of money on printing costs and postage.

AUTORESPONDERS

Some may equate autoresponders with those nearly useless instant-reply messages you receive whenever you send an e-mail to a company (i.e., "Thank you for your question. Someone will reply to you within 2 business days"). Actually, they can often be effective in that they can be used as an extra arm to maintain contact with the customer. Anytime you are asked to send information, an autoresponder can do that for you.

Web Ad.vantage lists these benefits of autoresponders:

- Knowing who has requested your information
- Reducing site visits
- Tracking response rates and interest levels of your offers
- Automating follow-ups and reminders
- Saving time in sending repetitive information

Tips to remember when using e-mail for marketing:

- Do ensure that each and every e-mail is responded to promptly. Once an e-mail address is advertised, it can be very difficult to navigate through the flood of messages. But it is very important not to ignore or delay an answer to a prospective customer.
- Do send positive and informative e-mails. Every single e-mail message that leaves your office is part of the overall marketing message.
- Do not send unwanted (or spam) e-mail messages. These messages are often ignored or responded to with a negative message. Instead, send mass messages using list serves or mail lists.

Measuring Success

Before you can measure the success of your electronic event marketing campaign, you need to decide what you will measure your success against. This can be determined by reviewing your original goals and objectives. Try also reexamining two areas: placement and the creative aspect. With placement, consider: Is this approach working for my organization? Is it bringing me more traffic?

Along the creative line, think about the actual ad or e-mail you are sending. Is this message working for me? Remember that an ad or message might work well with one audience, but not another; on one particular Web site, but not another. Microsoft's Bcentral.com gives a good analogy: If you are promoting Christmas ornaments, an ad for a football ornament may do well on a sports Web site, but not on a religious one. So be sensitive to the need to change your message if necessary as you change your target audience.

Things to consider when measuring the results of an electronic event marketing campaign:

- Total traffic
- Number of leads generated
- Percentage of leads converted into registrations/ticket sales
- Actual ticket sales/RSVPs
- Projected repeat customers

When deciding what to measure, carefully select the criteria. While it's easy to measure the "click-through" traffic, sometimes that isn't the best method to follow. For example, if you had a very catchy event banner ad, you may be getting a high volume of click-through traffic, which would look like a good investment. But if these clicks are not generating any action, they might not be effective.

A good way to decide what to measure is to decide what your goal is. Are you trying to bring more traffic to your site? Then measure click-through traffic. Are you trying to get more customers? Then measure e-mail sign-ups. Are you trying to sell a product? Then measure sales from an ad or e-mail message.

Banner advertisements tend to lose their effectiveness after a few weeks on the same site. You may consider alternating a variety of ads on the same site so viewers do not get bored. Another method to test may be running two different ads on the exact same site and then comparing the results to see which was more effective.

Once you have decided what you want to measure, it is time to determine which particular marketing campaign was the best at helping achieve your goal. This is when you would consider continuing the same campaign or if it is time to tweak and reeval-uate your ad and/or message. You may also consider comparing the return on your money—the sales per dollar spent—on each site. Do you increase or decrease your efforts?

Don't forget to review your entire online event marketing ef-forts. This includes e-mail marketing leads and search engines, as well as your affiliate marketing program. Should you increase your affiliates? Spend more time on adding your site to search en-gines? Add more ezines to your marketing list? Since this is a lot to consider, it may be helpful to have a professional strategist as-sist you in making your online marketing decisions.

Feedback is also invaluable. Through surveys and focus groups, you can find out how viewers perceived your site.

POSTCLICK TRACKING

Internet advertising can be measured by looking at the "click-through rate" on an Internet ad. The click-through rate is the per-centage of people who click the ad. As mentioned earlier, the click-through rate is usually less than 1 percent. You can measure the approximate cost of an ad by taking the total cost of the ad and dividing it by the number of times that someone clicked the ad. These figures will produce the "cost per click."

HAVING A ROUTINE

Once you have done research and created your marketing plan, take a deep breath and start again. Then begin the process of de-veloping your marketing "routine." A marketing plan is an essen-tial tool, but until you develop the "routine" to implement it, the marketing strategy is not complete.

Below is a very simple "mock plan" developed by Jim Daniels of JDD Publishing. His site **http://www.bizweb2000.com** has helped thousands of people profit online.

Daily

- Answer E-mail. This should be a number-one priority. In cy-berspace, people expect instant answers.
- Perform one marketing-related task. Big or small, make a pledge to perform a daily task, whether it is registering your

site on a new search engine or simply posting a message on a bulletin board.

Weekly

- Add a new page to your event Web site. Adding pages increases your exposure by allowing more points of entry, as well as by keeping your site fresh. This will ensure your customers don't find your site static or boring.
- Add a dozen or so search terms to your GoTo account.

Monthly

- Submit any new Web pages to at least five new search engines. Once you are listed on the major engines (e.g., AltaVista, Yahoo!, and Excite), move to the next level, among which are MetaCrawler, and LookSmart. Also, don't forget to be listed with multiengine searches such as Dogpile.com. You should be listed with as many search engines as possible.
- Identify one new ezine to consider for an ad placement. Placing advertisements in ezines is one of the greatest bargains available on the Internet. Your advertising cost can often be recovered after receiving one or two registrations.
- Write and submit an article to a targeted ezine publisher.

Quarterly

- Establish one completely automated marketing tool.
- Sign on one joint venture or partnership.

There are many companies that strive to improve online measuring techniques:

Accrue: **http://www.accrue.com**
Andromedia: **http://www.andromedia.com**
MatchLogic: **http://www.matchlogic.com**
Internet Profile: **http://www.ipro.com**
Media Metrix: **http://www.mediametrix.com**

Summary

In the relatively new world of electronic event marketing, the technologies and applications (not to mention the industry jargon) can be daunting to the uninitiated. If you, as a marketer, cannot do it right, find qualified professionals to do it for you or don't do it at all. Outdated product information, ineffective reader response features, and lack of follow-up will frustrate and deter buyers. E-commerce can be a double-edged sword. Make certain that whoever holds that sword knows how to use it.

The most critical elements of event Web site design are structure, ease of navigation, style, technical requirements, consistency, and personalization.

The selection of an event domain name, and your keywords, are integral to the ability of others to easily locate your organization through the myriad of search engines now plying the Internet on behalf of those looking for information about your event. The opportunities for electronic promotions are exploding as rapidly as the Net itself. Partnerships and cross-promotions have become commonplace through links, banner ads, tower ads, and co-endorsements. The key to measuring the success of your electronic event marketing effort is the availability of tracking systems, including your per month traffic, ad click-through statistics, and overall traffic data on the Web site offering the advertising to determine the site's viability in your marketplace.

TALES FROM THE FRONT

A small regional association sought ways to present itself as equal to the "big boys," and determined that an effective way to do that was to develop a home page for the organization. The staff member in charge of marketing brought the concept to the attention of the CEO, saying that this was the promotional wave of the future, and they were being left out. "No Web presence, no respect," was his argument. The CEO agreed, asking the marketer to investigate options and report back. What the boss did not know was that the marketer had a friend who had established a small Web site design and maintenance company. The concept had originated with his friend, who ob-

viously wanted the site design business. He offered a low price and high promises. And his design concepts were very promising. The CEO approved the plan.

The organization had its home page on the Web in short order. It was preceded by significant promotion, proclaiming the availability and excitement of the site and the opportunity for all to keep daily contact with the association through the Internet as well as enjoy the latest information without waiting for the mail or placing phone calls. "Exciting" and "current" were the watchwords of the promotion.

At first, it was exciting and current for the proud members. But, as time went by, nothing changed in the presentation. The design remained the same, no additional features were added, and the news was not from yesterday. It was from last summer. The site was no longer exciting and certainly not current. Coverage of the annual convention was literally last year's convention, overlapped by the most recent one. Leadership identifications were not updated. Features were old, many of which had not been changed since the association's Web site had been founded. The small Web site designer was capable of designing the site, but incapable of *maintaining and updating* it. With no such Web expertise on the as-sociation's staff, the site was stagnant and an embarrassment to the organization. After two years in the quandary, the small association bit the bullet and spent more money than budgeted to hire a design company with a track record for dynamic, current, and interactive home page applications.

The lessons?

You get what you pay for. Don't trust your professional reputation to friends with little money and little experience. And, remember this admonition: "Instead of crying over spilled milk, go and milk another cow."

Chapter Challenge

1. Design an electronic event marketing strategy for an event of your choice.
2. Write an effective e-mail message to use for an e-mail broadcast campaign.
3. Design your event Web page(s) and select a high-impact domain name.

CHAPTER 4

Funding the Event Marketing Program

It's the Budget, Stupid!

WHEN YOU HAVE COMPLETED THIS CHAPTER, YOU WILL BE ABLE TO:

- Develop the event marketing budget
- Identify resources to fund the budget
- Identify potential sponsors to support your budget
- Calculate the rate of return on event marketing

Developing the Budget

In its most basic form, a budget is your cash plan. It is how you are going to develop your mission and vision statements and your goals and objectives into reality financially. Don't let the budget become a burden. A budget should never be etched in stone; it is the final bottom line that counts. That being said, *never* attempt to manipulate your budget to cover expense overages or revenue shortfalls. A budget is fluid, but the adjustments should be made after careful analysis of the entire project.

To help in this analysis and in developing specific budget points for the marketing activities, there are some basic ideas that must be kept in mind initially. First, and foremost, everything has a price attached. Although this premise may sound elementary, it is often the small financial details that are overlooked that will have a huge impact on your marketing activities. Forgetting the price of postage to mail your 5,000 invitations can quickly erode any profit margin. Price doesn't necessarily have to be a monetary outlay; it could be an in-kind contribution or a barter/trade-out. Regardless of the type of transaction, the price has a value associated with it that impacts your budget on both the revenue and the expense sides.

The other two basic ideas to keep in mind while developing a budget are equally important to one another: price and cost. As you develop your budget, remember that *price* is the value placed on a good or service, while *cost* is what you sacrifice in the future by paying the price for a good or service today. An example would be if an organization pays $5,000.00 (the price) for a one-time print advertisement for an event, which may render the cost as insufficient funds to pay for radio spots in the future.

When developing the event marketing budget, there are several major financial categories to consider:

- Advertising
- Printing
- Postage
- Public relations
- Auxiliary opportunities
- Promotional printing

Each of these categories can, in turn, have many components, as shown in Figure 4-1. As you can see in Figure 4-1, there is overlap in the budget subcategories; several of the categories have postage and creative expenses related to them. To help identify these expenses, it is important that each category be assigned its own account code. Figure 4-2 helps clarify expenses in terms of category and type.

Advertising	Creative/Design Production Print TV Radio Web
Printing	Creative Graphic Design Mechanical Cost Couriers Printing Cost
Postage	First Class First Class Bulk Bulk Express
Consulting Fees	Marketing Specialists
Public Relations	Creative Writing Copying Press Releases Electronic
Auxiliary Opportunities	Promotional Booth/Stand
Promotional Printing	Banners and Posters Giveaways (T-shirts, mugs, etc.)

Figure 4-1

A broad marketing budget will include all categories that may incur expenses. This chart illustrates that many of the expenses will be reflected in more than one category. Examples are postage and couriers and creative (art and graphics) costs.

Finally, when developing a budget plan, there are three areas that are frequently overlooked:

1. Contingency reserve plans
2. Indirect costs (overhead)
3. Profit

Opinions differ on the amount of the overall budget needed to be set aside for a contingency plan, although between 10 and 20

Main Account Category	Subcategory	Account Number
Advertising 100	Creative/Design	100–101
	Production	100–102
	Print	100–103
	TV	100–104
	Radio	100–105
	Web	100–106
Printing 200	Creative	200–201
	Graphic Design	200–202
	Printing Cost	200–203
	Mechanical Cost	200–204
	Couriers	200–205
Postage 300	First Class	300–301
	First Class Bulk	300–302
	Bulk	300–303
	Express	300–304
Consulting Fees 400	Marketing Specialists	400–401
Public Relations 500	Creative	500–501
	Writing	500–502
	Copying	500–503
	Press Releases	500–504
	Electronic	500–505
Auxiliary Opportunities 600	Promotional Booth/Stand	600–601
Promotional Printing 700	Banners and Posters	700–701
	Giveaways (T-shirts, mugs, etc.)	700–702

Figure 4-2

Assigning account codes allows the marketer to understand the definitive amounts allocated to each expense category. The same account codes should be used for subsequent events, providing meaningful comparisons and financial evaluation.

percent is customary. You may ask, "If I have done my research and thought through the marketing strategy, why do I need a contingency plan?" The answer is simple. Unless you have a psychic on staff, you can't possibly know what will happen in the 10 or 18 months leading up to the event.

Ernst and Young, in their book *The Complete Guide to Special Event Management,* state that marketing is the most expensive

---

Projected Net Profit/Total Marketing Budget (Marketing Assets) = ROEM

Figure 4-3
An evaluation of the event's return on event marketing is critical
to ensuring that marketing activities are not negatively impacting
the profitability of the event.

item on the expense side of your budget. Therefore, it is imperative that you carefully research the price of each line item so it
does not adversely affect the event's overall bottom line. During
the budget development process, you must reevaluate your marketing strategy for the event to ensure fiscal soundness for your
plan. During this phase of development, you need to evaluate the
rate of return on event marketing (ROEM). To establish your ROEM,
use the formula shown in Figure 4-3.

For example, if the projected net profit for an event is $40,000
and the marketing assets are $280,000, then the ROEM is 14 per-
cent (40,000/280,000=.14). There is no set "magical" number for
an event to be viable from a marketing standpoint. Each event has
to be analyzed to determine if the ratio of marketing expense to
event profitability is worth the resources to continue. When considering the ROEM, the higher the ROEM percentage, the more financially viable the event becomes (see Figure 4-4).

ROEM = Financial Viability		
Projected Net Profit	**Marketing Assets**	**ROEM**
$19,250.00	$275,000.00	7%
$41,250.00	$275,000.00	15%
$55,000.00	$275,000.00	20%

Figure 4-4
The financial philosophy of the organization and the overall
goals of the event will determine the desired ROEM. A rule of
thumb is that the ROEM "sweet spot" for most marketers is
approximately 15 percent.

Identifying Funding Resources

Now that you have identified your budget needs for your marketing plan on the expense side, you have to cover those expenses through revenue. There are three revenue areas from which to draw:

- Internal
- External
- Client

Internal Sources
Cash reserves (advanced as seed money)
Discounts (organizational bulk purchasing power can lower the overall price paid for a product or service)

External Sources
"Loss leaders"
Ticket sales
Merchandising
Licensing
Loans—lines of credit with lenders
Concessions
Donations
Vendors
Sponsorship
Promotional partnerships
Back-end revenue—selling attendee mailing list, for example

Client
The event covers all expenses. The event may recoup investment through the use of external sources. Sometimes this type of funding is called "HIC," or "hope it comes," funding.

Usually, you will see a combination of these sources used on the revenue side of the event budget. It is not uncommon for an entity to undertake the financial liability for an event (internal or client) and then recoup that expense through external sources such as a loss leader. A loss leader is basically taking the risk of losing revenue in one area, such as providing complimentary or discounted registration fees to increase buyer attendance, in order to increase exhibitor demand, greater booth sales, and enhanced net income.

An existing or long-running event will have a budget item for cash reserves, which allows the event to continue to operate with a cash resource from year to year. A start-up event will need to obtain the seed money from either the client or an internal source, with the understanding that the funding will be repaid with the first revenues from external sources.

Identifying Sponsorships to Financially Support Your Event

According to the International Events Group or IEG, Inc. of Chicago, Illinois, sponsorship is the fastest growing form of marketing. It is estimated that, in 2001, entities from around the globe will spend over $24.6 billion to sponsor a variety of events, almost quadrupling the amount spent in 1998 (see Figure 4-5). Sponsorship is fast becoming the fourth arm of marketing, in addition to advertising, promotions, and public relations. Although sports events still dominate the types of events sponsored, there has been a steady increase in other categories such as arts, causes, festivals, and entertainment tours. Figure 4-5 details the amount of money spent in 1998 for event sponsorships.

Type of Event	Amount (U.S. $)	Percentage of Sponsorship Dollars
Arts	413 million	6%
Causes	544 million	8%
Festivals, Fairs, Annual Events	578 million	9%
Entertainment Tours	675 million	10%
Sports	4.55 billion	67%
Total	6.8 billion	
Source: IEG, Inc.		

Figure 4-5
While sports has long been the leader in attracting sponsors, other types of events are attracting increasing amounts of sponsorship dollars. This is a direct result of the greater awareness created by effective marketing.

Before you begin to identify potential sponsors that would be a fit for your event and marketing strategy, it is important to remember that sponsorship is neither benevolence nor philanthropy. While you can have both, sponsorship and philanthropy (donors), to support the revenue side of your budget, each is a very distinct entity. While philanthropic gifts are given out of a sense of altruism, sponsors are looking for a return on their investment (ROI). It is important to distinguish this type of revenue, as it will help in identifying potential sponsors. Another distinction that needs to be made in identifying potential sponsors is the type of event. This is particularly important when you begin to eliminate potential sponsors from your list based on their corporate policy of types of events they do and do not sponsor. According to Steve Jeweler and Julia Rutherford Silvers, authors of Event Sponsorship for the George Washington University Event Management Certificate Program, the following are among the types of events that seek sponsors:

- Hallmark, civic, and annual events
- Festivals and cultural events
- Sports events
- Meetings, conferences, and educational events
- Entertainment events, tours, and attractions
- Corporate cross-promotions
- Trade shows and expositions
- Cause-related events

With this understanding, you can then begin to identify the types of sponsors you are seeking:

- **Title/Presenting.** Underwrites a majority of the event.
- **Host/Supporting.** Underwrites specific areas of an event such as bars or food and beverage.
- **Tiered.** Monetary level determines the amount of exposure of sponsors' products, services, and individual leaders.
- **In Kind.** Often overlooked, in-kind sponsors provide their goods or services at no cost to the event for the sponsorship level related to the retail cost of the goods or services provided.

Once you have decided on the type of sponsor—or, more likely, the combination of sponsors—you can begin your research into entities that are interested in sponsorships and are a match with the audience and type of event you are producing. When you begin to brainstorm for potential sponsors, you must be aware that sponsors are everywhere; they are not located just among the large multinational corporations but also can be found at the corner store. Do not eliminate sponsors from your list because you think they are too small. Depending on the size and scope of the event, it is sometimes more cost effective to have several smaller sponsors than one or two large sponsors. You must remember when you are looking for sponsorship one of the first rules of thumb in budgeting is that everything has a price. This includes sponsorships. Again, the sponsorship is not a donation. It is a business deal where you are agreeing to promote the sponsors' goods and/or services in return for the value of your event to them. Not only does the servicing of this agreement have a price tag that impacts the expense side of your budget, it also has costs associated with it. Budgetary issues then become one of the first items to review when looking at potential sponsors. Is the ratio of expense to revenue to service the agreement worth the effort to secure the sponsorship?

The next step when working with an organization to develop potential sponsors is to ask "Who are your friends?" and "What are their interests?" The best opportunity to develop a relationship with a potential sponsor is to already know someone involved with the sponsor. Organizations may not even realize the potential

Who Are Your Friends?

Several years ago, a client was looking for sponsorships for a start-up charity sports event to help fund a nonprofit foundation. In the initial meeting, the client was overwhelmed with the finances needed to undertake the task of building a first-time event from the ground up. The question, "Who are your friends?" was asked. It turned out that the client's next-door neighbor was the CEO of a software firm that deeply believed in the work this nonprofit foundation did. He was more than happy "to help out" by not only signing on as a sponsor but endorsing the project in referrals to other firms with which his company did business.

sponsors with which they are already familiar and enjoy both organizational and personal relationships.

Your best starting point is doing an internal and external audit of all the stakeholders (those with a stake in the success of the enterprise) referrals from within your team and from within the organization looking for potential sponsors. In working with nonprofit entities looking for sponsorship, it is almost always the case that there is someone within the organization who knows somebody at XYZ Corporation. This can be a great help in getting that first sponsorship. However, most events will need more than one sponsor, and so we move on to the next step in identifying potential sponsors.

Research

The value of research cannot be stressed enough when you are identifying potential sponsors. Without proper research of companies' values, core concepts, and marketing strategies, you are bound to fail in an attempt to secure sponsorship. If you don't have a researcher on staff, hire one, even if it's on a part-time basis. A researcher finding that a CEO or president of a company has a favorite pastime, hobby, or cause has developed many sponsorship relationships. If you need to do the research yourself, here is a partial list of media to use to search for potential sponsors:

Daily newspapers
Periodicals
- Generic—*People, Vanity Fair, Newsweek*
- Product/service specific—*Sports Illustrated, Business Week*
- Special event
Advertising agencies
Internet search engines
Community public affairs office

Your research should also include the information needed to qualify any potential sponsors. What, if anything, have they sponsored in the past? Are they currently sponsoring any events? Your research should also determine the marketing strategy of the company, including the company's goals and objectives and the manner in which it might match the goals and objectives of your event. Emphasizing once again, sponsorship is a business deal, not a handout. It is support with commercial incentives; consequently, it is important during your research phase to make sure that the entity sponsoring your event doesn't have any hidden agenda that would be detrimental to the event organization. Finally, your research should verify the economic viability of the potential sponsor. The marketer must make certain that the sponsor has the financial means to back this business arrangement. To qualify your prospective sponsors, follow the steps in Figure 4-6.

You will have compiled your "short list" of potential sponsors that you have qualified as candidates for sponsoring your event. The next step in the process is to develop your approach strategy for each sponsor. Because potential sponsors have their own needs, wants, and desires, when approaching them you must create an individualized appeal. The prospectus should delineate how your

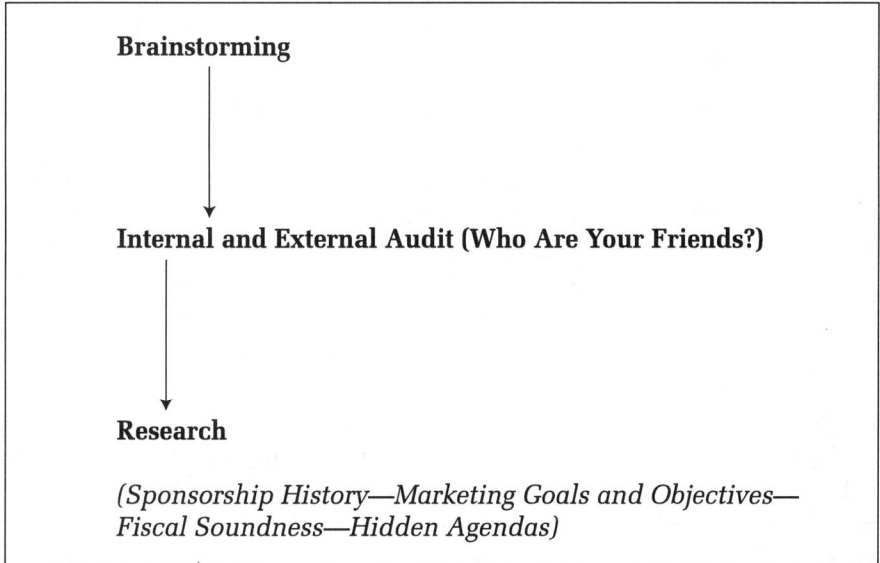

Figure 4-6
Event marketers often find the most loyal sponsors closest to home. Members, exhibitors, wholesalers, and distributors are among those who are already committed and who have a financial stake in the welfare of the event organization.

marketing plan blends with theirs, detail their potential return on investment, and list incentives for them to become sponsors.

Calculating Return on Sponsorship Investment

Sponsors want, and expect, a quantifiable return on the money they have invested in your event. As the event producer, you also need this information to enhance your ability to attract larger sponsorships in the future.

According to the IEG's *Complete Guide to Sponsorship,* there are three broad methods to evaluate the return on investment (ROI for the sponsor):

- Measuring awareness levels achieved or attitudes changed about the sponsor's products or services
- Measuring increase in sales of sponsor's products or services
- Comparing sponsor-driven media coverage to the price/cost of equivalent advertising

In the first two methods, the sponsor must follow certain requirements. To measure awareness levels or attitudes changed, the sponsor needs to have a presponsor level of awareness or consumer attitude about the sponsoring corporation and its goods or services. The sponsor also needs to maintain the current level of marketing of its goods or services so that it doesn't influence the outcome of the ROI. Finally, the sponsor must decide which objectives it wishes to measure, such as increase in sales, increase in brand awareness, and consumer attitude change, and should attempt to track only one variable at a time.

Measuring brand awareness or attitude change is done through either a survey or a focus group. The sponsor has to have a preevent level of branding to compare to the level of awareness both during and after the event. This type of measurement is typically used for sponsors with a long-term commitment to the event and is done over several event cycles. The sponsor needs to have defined goals as to the amount or percentage increase that it desires in brand awareness or attitude toward the brand.

There are many choices on which a sponsor may focus in measuring sales, beyond the obvious of increasing the sales of its goods or services to the consumer. A sponsor may also want to track an increase in distribution channels, generate better positioning at point-of-sale displays, produce new leads in a niche market or lifestyle market, or increase the volume of sales to current users. According to IEG, some of the methods that the sponsor can utilize to measure these types of increases in sales are:

- Comparing sales for a specific time around the event to previous years
- Comparing sales in the geographic area of the event to national averages in similar markets
- Analyzing proof-of-purchase promotions (discount tickets with proof of purchase or discount purchase with ticket coupon)
- Tracking increase in distributors before and during the event

Finally, the sponsor can measure the amount of media coverage that the event generates. By tracking the amount of time the event has exposure on radio and television as well as column inches in print media, the sponsor can assign a value to this exposure in comparison to what the price of this exposure would have been to buy outright. The sponsor may also be interested in the type of media exposure, national news versus the local six o'clock news, and mention in a national publication versus the local weekly newspaper.

Incentives to Attract Sponsors

Besides the return on investment, event sponsors look for other incentives that will increase their exposure at events and help with their overall marketing strategy. Some very effective incentives include:

- Media buys
- Cross-promotions
- Hospitality events
- Product samples
- Consumer research

Media buys allow sponsors to buy advertising to promote their affiliation with the event and any sales promotions that are running in conjunction with the event. An even greater incentive to the sponsor would be for the organization to buy a block of time and resell it to the sponsor at a discounted price.

Cross-promotional opportunities allow sponsors to work together to market to niche or lifestyle markets. An example of this type of promotion would be a sporting goods company and a sports drink company combining their efforts; with proof of purchase from the sporting goods company, the consumer would receive a coupon for a free sports drink. (*Research Note:* This is an excellent example of why research is so important. The creative marketer will look for these types of opportunities while doing research to increase his or her sponsorship potential.)

Hospitality opportunities are probably the largest incentive for potential sponsors. The opportunity to entertain either clients or staff allows the sponsor the chance to increase market share in existing markets, build new relationships, or thank employees and distributors. These types of activities can run the entire range, including a private hospitality tent, cocktail party, VIP seating, parking passes, or special valet parking. Any activity that is special to the sponsors and makes the event more enjoyable for them and their guests is an added incentive.

The ability of a corporation to utilize your event for passing out product samples, whether an existing product or a new product rollout, is a value-added incentive. Along with consumer research, it allows the corporation a direct contact with the consumer. It can also help establish a new consumer database through information gathered as a result of on-site surveys.

The more incentives that you can offer a potential sponsor, the better the chances that you will seal the deal. As with all business arrangements, each party is looking for the best possible advantage. Through the use of incentives, you can offer value added to that which the sponsor receives.

Nonfinancial Resources

An area of event sponsorship that is sometimes grossly overlooked is that of nonfinancial sponsors, or in-kind sponsors. This type of sponsorship is particularly appealing to new or small business en-

> ## A Win-Win Situation
>
> Two nonprofit clients have not paid for centerpieces for
> their annual fundraising dinners in the past year. They
> were matched to a florist and designers who supported
> their causes and thought they couldn't afford the price of
> a sponsorship. By doing an in-kind sponsorship (also
> known as a trade-out), they could afford to trade prod-
> uct/service for the sponsorship. In both cases, the busi-
> ness entities increased their market share for very little
> expense, and, at the same time, the organizations saved
> thousands of dollars in centerpiece expenses.

tities as it allows them an inroad to markets that otherwise might
be unattainable for them. A new business might not have the capital to invest in a sponsorship but could supply its product;
the same is true of an existing but small business that has cash
flow committed to other activities. This type of sponsorship is particularly effective when working with cause-related nonprofit
organizations.

Summary

The budget is your cash plan to turn your event goals and objectives into reality. Through the use of careful analysis of price and
cost, you can develop the benchmarks that are important to the
overall marketing plan. This analysis also allows you to keep an
eye on the details and to ensure correct reporting of both revenue
and expenses.

Once the expense side of the budget has been determined, the
resource side of the budget can be developed, looking at internal,
external, and client input. To ensure that the event is fiscally viable at this stage, examine the return on event marketing. The
need for external resources then leads to the development of sponsorship programs. Because there is a vast difference between sponsorships and donations, you need to develop a sponsorship business plan. This plan includes identifying potential sponsors,
qualifying those sponsors to match your marketing goals and

objectives. You must then present to potential sponsors the benefits of their investment and encourage their sponsorship with additional incentives.

TALES FROM THE FRONT

A recent client, a nonprofit association in the healthcare field, decided to enhance its annual silent/live auction by soliciting sponsors. At its annual board retreat, my team and I took the board members step by step through the process of looking for and acquiring sponsors. At first, they had doubts about the idea of sponsorship. They thought they were too small an organization and that they had "nothing to offer" a potential sponsor. Every organization has something to offer! As we took board members through the process, they began to see that you don't have to be a major cause-related organization or a major event to attract sponsors. In fact, this organization runs a trade show prior to the auction and didn't realize with the right marketing they had potential sponsors already there. Once they realized "who their friends were," it became easier for them to envision other sponsors. My researcher, a college librarian, found new sources not only for potential sponsorship but also potential exhibitors for their trade show. It may not be of Olympic proportions but the extra revenue will allow this association to give three more scholarships this year.

Chapter Challenge

Prepare a marketing budget for a three-day jazz festival to be held on the waterfront of a second-tier city. The budget should include all expenses related to the marketing plan and discussion of their importance to the overall success of the event. The budget should also include, on the revenue side, the amount of revenue generated by internal, external, and client sources. Discuss the process of identifying potential sponsors and your method of approach. Finally, conduct an ROEM and explain why this event is or is not economically viable.

CHAPTER 5

Marketing Association Meetings, Conferences, Events, and Expositions

They Will Buy . . . When You Tell Them Why!

WHEN YOU HAVE COMPLETED THIS CHAPTER, YOU WILL BE ABLE TO:

- Understand the unique nature of association structure, leadership, and operational patterns
- Appreciate the special challenges of association event marketing
- Identify techniques for effective list management
- Compare promotional methods and their effectiveness for specific audiences
- List the dos and don'ts of brochure design and production
- Recognize the differences between internal and external public relations
- Establish incentive strategies for both exhibit sales and attendance growth

The Association: A Unique Business Model

THE CHALLENGES AND OPPORTUNITIES OF CONVENTION AND EXPOSITION MARKETING

When marketing events for trade associations, professional societies, and philanthropic organizations, the responsibility for selling their events mandates a clear understanding of the unique nature of volunteer organizations. Unlike corporations, the characteristics of which will be discussed in the next chapter, associations and societies are volunteer driven. Certainly, the association's staff is likely salaried, but the organization is driven by elected or appointed volunteer leaders, with final authority over staff activities and effectiveness.

Why is this important to the marketing executive? The reason is that effective sales and marketing depends on a clear definition of the goals and priorities of the sponsoring organization. Only then can the "why" of the five Ws be defined. However, because associations are guided by elected and appointed officials who volunteer their involvement, their terms of office are finite and goals and objectives may be subject to frequent change as leaders come and go. Think of national or state elections. A new president or governor brings in new appointees, new concepts, and new priorities. The same is true of association elections and evolvement. As a matter of fact, many elected presidents proudly refer to their term of office as "my year." They want to leave their mark.

As a marketer of association events, should you care about the organization's politics? Understand the event and sell it. That should be enough, right? But it isn't!

The organization's goals and objectives, as well as those of the leadership, are paramount in developing marketing strategies. For example:

- Does the association now wish to reach out to other organizations for cross-promotional purposes?
- Has the financial goal for its events changed from "break even" to "make a profit"?
- Has the emphasis or character of the annual meeting changed

from fellowship, fun, and conviviality to education and idea sharing?

- Does the new president want to be featured as the cornerstone of the event, unlike her predecessor who wished to remain in the background?
- Is this event intended to proclaim dramatic changes in organizational structure, as well as plans for a new headquarters building?
- Will the coming year be dedicated to new alliances with industry entities, the momentum for which will be developed at the annual convention?

The point is that marketing strategies must reflect the priorities favored by elected leadership and paid staff, and those association priorities may be much more fluid than will usually be found with corporate events, the leadership of which is more entrenched. That being the case, the corporation's goals are typically more identifiable—namely, please the shareholders (stakeholders) and energize and reward the employees.

STAKEHOLDERS

Stakeholders for any event can be described as those who hold a personal and compelling interest in the success of that event. For an association, stakeholders clearly will include board and committee members, staff, event attendees, and exhibitors. Look even further, however, for other stakeholders who rely on marketing for a successful and well-attended event that will fill their needs and expectations. These will include suppliers (e.g., event facilities, caterers, transportation companies, exhibit designers and decorators, speakers, entertainers, and security companies). And examining even further, local merchants, host-city attractions, labor union personnel, the convention bureau, and the chamber of commerce certainly have a stake in an attendance-rich event.

And how does that happen? It happens through a combination of pertinent programming and *creative marketing*. The greatest challenge? Understanding the *purpose* of the event and the organizational goals that have been identified by elected leadership and salaried staff. The greatest opportunity? Translating those priorities and the association's "corporate culture" into creative marketing strategies that will bring association goals to life as the target audience learns *why* they should buy the tickets and participate. When they do that in large numbers, stakeholders will be pleased, and the marketing professional will be asked to return and repeat that great performance next year!

An illustration of a sampling of association audiences, along with some ideas on the communications messages that should be considered for the marketing strategies, appears in Figure 5-1.

Model for Marketing Communications Strategies

(Audiences and Messages to Be Considered)

Event: →

Stakeholders: *Politics, Support, Corporate Culture*

New Attendees: *Researching Expectations, Creating Awareness, Initiation into Association Purposes*

Related Associations: *Cross-Promotions, List Sharing, Speaker Exchange*

Sponsors: *Levels of Financial Support, Recognition, Benefits of Sponsorship*

Exhibitors: *Rules and Regulations, Terms of Booth Assignment, Plans to Increase Traffic*

Speakers: *Speakers' Information Kit, Profile of Audience, Invitation to Attend All Events*

Elected Leadership: *Personal Preferences, Individual Recognition, Association Issues*

Figure 5.1
Crafting the messages aimed at specific association constituencies will enhance marketing communications. Research into each target market is essential in understanding the needs and major areas of interest inherent among them.

Promotion Methods
for Association Events

A detailed list of promotional tools appears in Chapter 2. Virtually all these campaign methods may be considered for association meetings and events, but certain ones will be rejected because of the nature and marketing needs of the event, the cost effectiveness of the promotional approach, the range of the markets to be reached, and the political/psychographic preferences of management. However, the following are classic tools for membership organizations to use in their event marketing campaigns.

DIRECT MAIL

The mail campaign will be effective and affordable only if the list management is efficient. Associations normally rely on staff for list management. List maintenance (updating and verifying the accuracy of mailing lists) may be performed internally or may be outsourced to a list maintenance contractor.

List management involves the surveys, analyses, and tracking of members, associate members, elected leadership, sponsors, exhibitors, and all others who would like to remain—or become—stakeholders in the event. This involves continuous research:

- Change-of-address reminders on membership renewals and as inserts in other mailings
- Return change-of-address postcards in association periodicals
- Monitoring of industry publications for news about employee movement and additional prospects
- Change-of-membership data forms for association chapters and allied organizations
- Mailings to "dropped-member" archival lists, to solicit information on the potential new member or his or her most recent location
- Telemarketing campaign to the most recent stakeholder contact location to update information
- Records-update forms conveniently located with a drop box at registration desks at all organizational events, meetings, and expositions, as well as at chapter events

- Cross-comparisons with related society and association membership directories
- Name/address/phone number "correction-alert" self-mailer in the association's annual membership directory
- "Broadcast fax" requests for updated information
- Instant-response feature on the association's Web site, as well as industry electronic bulletin boards
- Review of chapter membership directories
- Review of addresses on checks received
- Review of supplier records, ads, and press releases
- Review of your own address book

The list could go on ad infinitum. Often, mailing lists are updated simply by one's being alert to casual information passed along about a stakeholder's change in station, title, or direct telephone number and e-mail address through a conversation with a friend. Write it down at that moment and deliver it to those who are responsible for updating the records and maintaining the lists.

List management also requires demographic/geographic segmentation. Effectively categorized, the marketing executive can maximize expense efficiency by minimizing wasted printing and postage for unwanted target markets. Depending on the amount of information gathered in the research for list management, computerized lists can be coded to include or exclude any number of variables, such as:

- By state(s)
- By title
- By professional discipline or trade sector
- By name
- By number of years of membership
- By elected leadership position(s)
- By number of events attended in the past, and years attended
- By ranking of advertising and sponsorship support
- By attendance at pre- and postevent tours and other ancillary events
- By attendance at previous association seminars or workshops
- By current-member, dropped-member, or potential-member status

(There is nothing more embarrassing than getting chewed out by a veteran convention attendee who received a "Come Get to Know Us" solicitation from the marketing department.)

Many marketers fall into the trap of mining the same old list year after year. Creativity calls for new concepts. Who else can benefit from this conference? Try a focus group approach for researching the answers to that question. Review occupational handbooks and industry directories. Ask suppliers for information about their client lists, those they would like to see attend your exposition.

Examine the offerings of list brokers and direct-mailing services for audiences who will be worth additional investment in the data they can provide. Meet with representatives of pertinent industry trade publications and professional journals to determine their subscriber readership in your field who may become potential attendees (as well as potential members). Inquire as to the availability and cost of subscription lists.

A periodic list management audit is fundamental to effective list maintenance. Among the questions that should be included are: "When was our list last formally updated?" "Could we use our list today for an immediate mailing or phone solicitation?" "What is the chain of command for ensuring that updated information is passed along and immediately incorporated into the list?" "What record keeping is in place to ensure that process has been accomplished, and with accuracy?"

This audit should not be taken as part of a casual conversation over the coffee pot, but rather as a continuous and candid formalized review of all staff involved. Given the continuing increases in the costs of postage, paper, printing, and labor, proficient marketers must treat list management with no less a sense of daily urgency and discipline.

What marketing vehicles are available through direct mail? Incredibly, most associations miss many of the most obvious. Direct mail, for example, is not necessarily limited to the promotional brochure that is *in* the envelope. It should also include the preprinted event message or slogan that is *on* the envelope. Every organizational mailing for months prior to a convention should bear a "teaser," or a reminder of the event, even before the recipient opens the envelope to find a business letter, an invoice, or a report about events in the legislature.

If preprinting is not an option, brightly colored stickers also work well to grab attention. They can be utilized on the association's envelopes and letterhead, the front sheet of press releases, monthly newsletters, mailings of meeting minutes, and virtually every other mailing piece generated toward the appropriate targets.

E-mail is becoming more predominant as a direct-mail tool. However, prudence requires that e-mail only be sent to those who are on an "opt-in" list. Sending out an e-mail promotion to those not inviting or wanting it is counterproductive. In the industry, this is called "spamming," which has become a word with a deeply negative connotation. "Opt-in" lists can be built by asking for e-mail addresses on registration (for updated conference information), on confirmation forms, at the event itself, and in membership literature. Many "opt-in" lists also provide the "opt-out" option for recipients who no longer want the information by e-mail, and can indicate so by clicking a hyperlink attached to the page.

There is no such thing as oversaturation of direct-mail reminders to create the image of the event, nurture and grow the message in the consciousness of the reader, and create the conversations and buzz in your target communities that will turn the dream of this event into reality.

BROCHURES

Priscilla Richardson is president of WriteSpeakforSuccess, (WriteSpeakforSuccess.com), a leading business communications company. Her work with associations and corporations in business writing, speaking, and marketing communications is known for its creative brochure design strategies.

Her first admonition: Sell the *benefit!* She cautions that marketers remember that the brochure must not be designed to please the marketer, but rather to attract the attendees. *What do they get when they buy?* Then differentiate between program benefits and program features. A feature, for example, is a component of the event. It may be four group meals, a key speaker, or an offering of seven seminars and two general sessions. A benefit, on the other hand, is *what your program will do for your attendees.* It starts with the actual or implied *"You."*

Marketing executives must remember that the event and the promotional materials are not about them. They are about the potential buyers. Benefits solve their problems, fulfill their potential, organize their lives and their offices, allow them to interact with others more effectively; increase their profits, or help them learn to speak effectively in public. The benefits offered in brochures should be predicated on the results of the quantitative and qualitative needs surveys discussed in Chapter 1.

Features, on the other hand, are the components of the program designed to deliver the benefits. While it is important to describe the features in the brochure, it is vital to make the benefits the front-page news of the brochure. Short, concise benefit descriptions can range from "You will write faster and more succinctly" to "You will gain increased profits with less stress" to "You will save hours every week."

Benefits command attention and induce action. Features then fill in the blanks and add icing to the cake.

Dr. Richardson adds these "three things never to do: Each one *guaranteed to kill potential attendee interest.*"

- *Only mention features.* Omit benefits.
- *Give the history of the organization or the event, including names and dates.*
- *Hide the registration information.* Make the reader play a game to find it. Or design your brochure so that if your registrant clips out the registration form, he or she will lose vital information needed later.

Tell Them What You're Going to Tell Them . . .
Then Tell Them . . .
Then Tell Them What You Told Them!
—Venerated principle for public speakers

This old principle for public speakers was the benchmark for assuring that the audience got the message. It is as simple as that. A lecturer or after-dinner speaker would begin by telling the listeners why he was speaking on a particular subject and what key issues were deserving of close attention. This was the "teaser." The presentation would follow, covering those issues as well as others. Then, in conclusion, the speaker would summarize the key points, perhaps with additional visual aids, and, in many cases, would solicit audience reaction, questions, and comments (another example of qualitative research).

Direct mail should be designed to follow that same principle for broadcasting your message. Here are some classic examples of how to do this.

Tell Them What You're Going to Tell Them. . .

This might take the form of a "teaser" mailing (a postcard or single sheet) containing the five Ws and urging the reader to "hold these dates!" It should contain at least a few of the benefits (not features) of attending. The teaser can be mailed well before event plans, speakers, and topics are finalized. It can be mailed months in advance of the meeting. Timing will depend on the nature of the market's need to know, advance notice required for business and personal calendars, and the scope of the event itself. The promise is "More to Come!" Many associations include this perfunctory information on the back cover of the event program book, even a year in advance.

Then Tell Them. . .

A preliminary brochure can be considered, even before final program components are in place. It serves as a reminder that the big event is in the planning stages and will be held on these dates, in this place. Often called "preliminary programs," this caveat offers the details in place to date and implies that more details will follow. Certain speakers may even be listed as "invited." Still, it continues to build interest and excitement in the event's benefits and features.

The final program brochure will tell the audience the full story, highlighting key points and benefits just as the principle of public speaking requires of the speaker. It will contain the benefits to be experienced by the attendee, prominently displayed on the cover. Other details are highlighted, including schedule, registration information, return forms, housing forms, travel information and forms, requests for special assistance or accommodations, speakers' bios, and any other relevant information. All of this should be graphically designed so that the clipping of forms for return to the registration office will not destroy program information needed later for review by the recipient.

Then Tell Them What You Told Them!

Use a follow-up mailing after the event to do some quantitative or qualitative research *and to promote the next event.*

Many marketers will offer an incentive for response, such as a reduced registration fee for that event or an invitation to a special leadership reception. Key to this mailing should be an emphasis on the highlights of the event being researched, with some photos and a listing of highly rated seminars.

An extremely effective vehicle to include as well are written testimonials from pleased and enthusiastic attendees. As discussed in Chapter 1, these testimonials can be gathered at the event itself through the qualitative research efforts or gathered later by telephone, in letters by appreciative attendees, or through personal conversations. Most people love to see their names in print to be read by peers and colleagues; nevertheless, permission to publish is essential before printing the follow-up mailing.

Brochure Graphics and Design

Once again for emphasis: *Sales start on the cover.* Bear in mind that a "brochure" can range from a single-sheet imprint on inexpensive paper, to a one-fold piece providing four printing surfaces, to a dramatic multifold, four-color brochure on glossy stock. Regardless, the sales message should also be included on the envelope, if the brochure is not designed as a self-mailer. The critical information once again includes the five Ws of marketing: *Who* (is holding the event)? *What* (is the title of the event)? *Where* (will the event be held)? *Why* (should one attend)? *When* (will the event be held)?

Benchmarks for Graphic Design

Although there are exceptions to the rules, these general benchmarks will be helpful to those who design event brochures:

1. The brochure should provide a contrast of dark type on light paper. "Drop-out" lettering, or white lettering on colored paper, may be pretty, but is difficult to read in any paragraph format.
2. Long paragraphs and verbose sentences will inhibit continued reading and interest. Use short, punchy sentences. Simple lists with bullets or numbers will catch the eye faster than a paragraph of complex sentences.
3. The writer should never do a final proofreading personally. If the author misses an error one time, the odds are great that he or she will miss it again. Have others proof in the final stages. The writer should want to know that readers are clear about the message and impressed by the wordsmanship. Proofreaders should be ensured that there is no

"pride of authorship" and their candid suggestions are appreciated.

4. Photographs should be incorporated effectively, to illustrate the gorgeous venue or the face of a famous keynote speaker. Photos without a purpose, or used simply to fill space, are often impediments to easy reading. Finally, clip art should not be used on major pieces. Readers know that it is a cheap computer contrivance, and that will make your brochure seem cheap as well.

5. All photographs, artwork, and illustrations must be used with the proper permission from creators or producers.

6. Type fonts should be used sparingly. Preferred is a font with a simple design that is large enough (never less than 10-point type for text) to be read easily by older readers. A change in type fonts can be used (e.g., between headlines and text), but the brochure designer should never use more than three fonts in a brochure. It will make the brochure look as though someone was playing around with the computer. (That's fun, but not effective!)

7. Bright, contrasting colors make for memorable, easily identifiable mailing pieces. Subtle combinations, such as pink type on a red background or light gray on a darker gray, may be an elegant combination but will likely not grab attention.

8. The reader should not be forced to search for the response mechanism. Make it easy to respond! The registration form, hotel reservation form, as well as hotel descriptions and rates, and airline/train/bus information should be placed prominently and must be usable without destroying important contiguous information that the attendee will want to review later. Also, critical response aids such as all telephone numbers, e-mail addresses, fax numbers, and other information needed for quick responses should be included on all registration/reservation forms. Additionally, it is imperative to include information for those who need to request special assistance for the handicapped.

9. Not all of the space need be filled with text or photographs. Blank areas (or "white space") should not be overdone, but a strategic allocation of white space will make the reading easier on the eyes.

10. Boxes (sometimes called a "box-all") or boldfaced sidebars are effective graphics used to emphasize special features or highlight a quote from a key speaker. This adds "color" to the page, even without the use of artwork.

11. Careful negotiations with the printer are essential to control the costs of the brochure design and printing. Every upgrade in paper stock, every additional fold or flap, will cost more in press time, paper, and labor. And discerning marketers are alert to cost issues when considering "die-cuts," or specialized decorative or custom shapes cut into the brochure's cover or folds. While very impressive, the procedure is also very expensive.

12. Prior to printing, the brochure should be developed into a "mock-up" for a panel of peers (a focus group) to proof one last time for clarity, spelling, and grammar. Then a review of overall attractiveness and effectiveness should follow. It is less expensive to make corrections at this stage, and much less embarrassing and costly than discovering mistakes at the print shop.

Finally, and to repeat, the event is not about you, it is about your *attendees* and the *benefits* that they will receive. Maintain that philosophy throughout the writing and production of the brochures. They will likely be a key element of the marketing strategy.

ADVERTISING

Many media alternatives exist for associations to weigh as they plan advertising for their events. Among the choices are those closest to home, as well as the least expensive. These are the association's own publications. Following are some organizational publications, house organs, and other advertising vehicles, which are often overlooked as possibilities:

- Association magazines and newsletters (the advertisements are often called "house ads," ready for insertion anytime and anywhere space is available)
- Membership promotional brochures
- Event program books (back-cover ad for upcoming event)
- Press and media kits for association legislative materials or other activities

- Promotional brochures for unrelated events such as a speakers' series or a special fundraiser
- Chapter and affiliate newsletters and magazines
- Letterhead and envelopes (preprinted or stickers)
- Membership directories (including those of allied groups)
- Association Web sites
- Closed-circuit television at organizational events
- Recorded message for those on "hold" for the headquarters telephone
- Tent cards for members' reception rooms

In other words, the savvy marketing executive will look at every piece of print material, electronic communication, and even seemingly unrelated association activities that may provide a vehicle for advertising the event. In most cases, except for the cost of developing and printing a "stock ad," the cost of ad insertion is free because the medium is association controlled. And, obviously, the audience will be that which is most sensitive to the message. This is the easiest audience segmentation available.

Stock ads are often preprinted on a reprographic, or "repro" sheet, photo-ready for the printer to use in any journal or newsletter. While various publications may use different column widths and page sizes, ads are generally produced to fit on an "as needed" basis and may often appear when the publisher needs a "fill" to eliminate white space and fill a page. Ad size adjustments can be made by the publisher or printing company by expanding or reducing the image. However, the normal increments for advertising (either purchased or free) are ¼ page, ½ page, ¾ page, and full-page inserts. Or, they may be designed in column inches at the direction of the publisher.

Regardless of whether or not advertising is paid or free, it is incumbent upon the writer/designer to maintain specific objectives and goals in the preparation of the ad. A good ad will contain several, or many, of the following desired principles, designed to convey the messages and the mission:

1. Creating a "stopping power" headline, designed to grab the attention of the reader
2. Using the language of the market, complete with "buzz words" and anecdotes that are quickly identifiable
3. Designing editorial content that conveys the image and spirit of the event

4. Targeting specific market segments, whether they are families, business executives, golfers, scientists, or schoolteachers; addressing their particular needs in the message
5. Stressing program innovations that will result in new and unique benefits to the attendee
6. Emphasizing program participation by key industry leaders, professional icons, or celebrities
7. Making it easy for the reader to respond, by listing phone and fax numbers, e-mail addresses, and Web site addresses

Incentives may also be used effectively with advertising. Discount coupons and deadlines for "early bird" registrations at reduced rates are easily included in print ads to drive early business and more accurately estimate attendance and guarantee requirements for the venue and the physical space required.

While not as commonplace as print advertising, the association event marketer should also consider other alternatives with a careful eye toward the budget. It is important to identify other media buying opportunities and integrate them into the overall marketing strategy. Beyond print advertising, additional options include electronic media such as radio, television, and cable as well as the Internet, plus outdoor advertising (from billboards to street banners) and specialty advertising. Many of these options are discussed in Chapter 2.

Regardless of the advertising vehicle selected, the marketer will want to develop separate budgets for all media. Television ads will likely fall into pricing categories based on 10-, 15-, or 30-second intervals. Radio broadcasters will also have their own advertising ranges, typically from 10-second to 1-minute spots. The most effective way to gauge the budget (and value) of various media approaches is to:

- Develop a separate budget for each medium.
- Identify other events of similar scope and study their media budgets.
- Study the history of the association's event and evaluate relative return on investment of the media utilized compared to previous years. If that historical information is not available, a system should be established for tracing the results of various advertising approaches (e.g., "hits" on the Web site, coupons from trade press ads, faxed registration forms, mailed registration forms, telephone orders, etc.).

Finally, if the budget allows, consideration could be given to hiring an advertising agency to develop advertising concepts and design, as well as a strategy for ad placement. This should be an agency well familiar with the association's industry or profession, as well as the meetings industry and the purpose of the type of event being promoted. While agency references should always be checked, an advertising agency with intimate knowledge of, and space-buying influence within an industry—as well as creative copy writers and graphic artists—can be a great asset to the advertising program.

PUBLIC RELATIONS

The purpose of public relations is to inform audiences, mold attitudes, and encourage participation. While it could be said that brochures and advertising do the same, there are some striking differences.

For example, while the results of advertising or direct mail are easily measurable, the results of public relations are more difficult to quantify. The reason? Advertising is what the event organization says about itself. Public relations results in what others *say and feel* about the organization and its event, the attitudes of which may be more diffuse and theoretical. Still, it remains an integral and critical part of the overall marketing strategy. Advertising is completely controlled by the marketer who buys it; he or she mandates the design, timing, placement, and message. With public relations, the buyer has no control.

Public relations campaigns run the gamut of building on success or overcoming failure. The campaign may be designed to reaffirm past successes of a winning event to advance it even further against the competition. Or a public relations effort may be designed to turn around a failing event and "spin" its strengths to gain an approving audience in the face of past adversities. This effort may include both internal and external public relations target markets.

Regardless, a public relations success usually provides more benefit for the investment than advertising or brochures, because the message does not come from the sponsoring organization but rather comes from a third party. The positive spoken word from a third party carries more credibility than the word of the sponsoring association, which carries on its sleeve its vested interests in the success of the event.

Internal Public Relations

For a trade association or professional society, the marketer should first seek resources internal to the organization itself. Where to look? Stakeholders. The board of directors, staff, committees, chapter leaders, past presidents, exhibitors, all of those who have an intrinsic interest in the success of the project. These are the people who are, at the least, somewhat interested and, at best, eager to assist in promoting the event.

The marketing executive may consider these tools for internal public relations for use by stakeholders:

1. Focus groups to determine candidly the attitudes of others and identify the most reliable resources to represent the cause.
2. Fact sheets, background articles, and press kit materials to make the stakeholders comfortable with past history and future plans.
3. Scripts for speeches to be delivered to members, chapter audiences, and allied or related associations.
4. Personal approaches, phone calls, and visits by association leaders to other "movers and shakers" in the industry to spread the word.
5. Videos to be distributed to chapters and related societies, for viewing and discussions at chapter and leadership meetings.
6. Advertisements for association publications with readerships pertinent to the campaign.
7. Press releases to trade publications.
8. "Advertorials" prepared for industry magazines and newspapers. Many such publications welcome editorial coverage of an event or production, which, in fact, may be a thinly veiled promotion of the value of the event and the sponsoring association. These are often run on a "space-available" basis.

External Public Relations (Creating an Awareness)

External public relations reaches beyond the association family and attempts to identify those who may not be intimately aware of the event but have supportive potential. They may become stakeholders when they understand what the event means to the organization and to the community they represent. For example, if the event is being held in a new location, the elected leaders, press, radio and television stations as well as the police and fire departments, transportation officials, and others can be included among those whose awareness must be raised. What can be done to achieve this? Again, fully armed with press kits, fact sheets, and all other pertinent organizational information:

1. Contact the *mayor's office.* Invite him or her to welcome the delegates at the opening session. Offer a full registration. Provide background information on the meeting and the organization's great contributions to society.

2. Meet with, or at least provide information to, local *politicians, community leaders,* and any others with high communicative access, and a high profile, in the area. Again, the purpose is to *create awareness.*

3. Meet with *fire and police officials* to discuss the fire marshal requirements for meeting and exhibit rooms. Provide police information regarding traffic patterns, and people movement, parade or street fair permits, and the general demographics of your attendees. While they will not help promote the meeting, the marketer can be assured they speak daily with the mayor's office and other city officials. Creating awareness comes from many directions.

4. Reach out to *labor union representatives.* If labor unions will be involved with the meeting (for exhibits, stagehands, trash removal, electricians, or other trades), a visit with union officials can create personal and civic awareness of the event and recognition of the organization, its plans, and its needs. Union officials are never reticent to discuss requirements, contracts, and rates with event planners. And because unions are often viewed in an adversarial role by convention planners, they appreciate the attention and recognition such personal inquiries bring to them.

5. Ensure that public relations efforts embrace the *convention bureau* in the host city. The more the convention bureau understands the nature of your event, the greater the chance of assistance in terms of both local information and public involvement. Many convention bureaus will provide brochures and other literature about area tourism features

and members whose facilities and services are available to your attendees. These resources provide excellent ancillary information with which to market the event. Moreover, the convention bureau typically moves with significant influence in city politics, giving the association an even greater presence and awareness among local decision makers.

6. Contact the local *chamber of commerce.* The chamber of commerce can be an excellent resource. An aggressive public relations campaign about the event, including buying power and demographics of attendees, can induce local merchants to display welcome signs in windows and provide discount coupons for their shops and restaurants for the association to distribute as an extra benefit to attendees.

Holding a Media Conference

A media or press conference is an excellent way to get the word out and establish relationships with those who can give you press coverage, accommodate ads and "advertorials" in their publications, and slot your public service announcements into their broadcast programming. There are a number of ways to determine whom to invite. A canvass of broadcast and print media information in the location of the event should begin with chamber of commerce and convention bureau membership lists and personal inquiries of local contacts such as members and supporters. Personal intervention by local association leaders can greatly enhance the opportunities for press and broadcast coverage. In general, news assignment editors at radio and television stations and city editors at newspapers will be the first contacts to gain attention. They may assign others to cover the media conference, depending on the nature of the subjects to be covered, such as business, sports, style, or entertainment.

These strategies should be observed when planning a media conference:

1. Locate the conference in as central a location as possible, with greatest proximity to the press and broadcast stations. This may be a hotel, press club, or a public hall.
2. Ask the members of the press about timing. Attempt to schedule for their convenience. For example, a television

station may prefer mid-morning, in order to have reports or interviews ready for the afternoon and evening news. By the next day, the report could well be old news for their editors. Newspapers may prefer midweek, because of the pressure of reporting on heavy weekend events during their Friday deadlines. The point is that the media representatives themselves can provide guidelines to the marketer that will help accommodate their schedules and maximize attendance. Avoid weekends and Mondays.

3. Have refreshments on hand, coffee, juices, light finger sandwiches, or croissants, and be sure to include this information in your invitations.

4. Be certain to determine that all who accept the invitation are accredited by their employer and properly credentialed with identification badges at the media conference registration desk.

5. If featured speakers are included in the conference, an appropriate stage and background should be provided with adequate lighting for television cameras and photography. Biographies of the speakers should be distributed in advance as well as on site. Other considerations are:

   - Appoint a moderator to provide introductions, field questions, and make certain that the session begins and ends at the prescribed times.
   - Provide clear lines of sight for cameras.
   - Make sure that speakers are briefed and rehearsed.
   - Include telephones, facsimile lines, copiers, Internet connections, and individual interview areas for major media conferences.

Exhibitor Marketing Techniques

Increasingly, many associations regard exhibitors as an integral part of the convention mix. Expositions open an essential avenue of communication between those who supply products and services to the organization and the association's member-buyers. Moreover, they provide a critical revenue stream to the organization through exhibit fees, sponsorships, and other types of support. In many cases, the revenue generated from exhibit sales will dwarf any of the other income sources needed to produce the overall event.

For example, DeWayne S. Woodring, executive director and CEO of the Religious Conference Management Association, says that his organization has not raised member registration fees for nearly two decades. Rather, he explains, the association has judicially grown the exposition (and the revenue it generates) in size and importance as a major convention component, assuring that the balance of buyers and sellers presents a viable market investment for exhibitors and a rich source of product information for the association's members.

He raises a key point. There must be an equitable balance between the number of exhibit booths sold and the buyers who attend the show. Lonely exhibitors and empty aisles are a daunting nightmare for exhibit managers and marketers.

When marketing exhibit space, these elements are paramount:

- History and growth of the show and its buyer attendance.
- Testimonials from exhibitors and buyers attesting to the economic viability of the event.
- Credibility and purpose of the sponsoring organization.
- "Qualifying" the association's buyer base, through quantitative and qualitative research. While numbers of people in the aisles are important, the exhibitors will want to know the profile of the potential buyers: their professional level, spending authority, specific product interests and needs, and demographic characteristics.
- Defining the role of exhibitors in the overall conference program. Are they welcome to attend seminars, social events, and general sessions? These are important opportunities for additional customer contact and value-added benefits of supporting the organization. Many association exhibitors who are relegated to restricted convention participation react negatively to the "second-class citizen" syndrome.
- Preparation of a clear and concise "exhibitor prospectus," outlining rules, regulations, and other requirements of exhibiting.

The Prospectus

A keystone of marketing is the prospectus. Usually drawn up as a team effort among management, marketing, and legal advisors, the prospectus may be a dazzling four-color brochure or a simple set of copied pages, depending on the scope of the exposition. The elements of a prospectus will vary from organization to organization as rules and regulations vary. Regardless, a number of items may be included so that exhibitors understand the terms of their agreement. Among them:

- Official show dates, location, and exhibit hours
- Comprehensive dates and hours, including setup and teardown deadlines
- Eligibility requirements
- Booth sizes
- Booth floor plan (with schematics and booth numbers)
- Booth costs (with inclusions, such as booth furnishings)
- Payment options, including deposits and final payment dates
- Liabilities and local covenants and restrictions
- Information about official contractors, including decorator, electrical, plumbing, telephone and Internet cabling, security, shipping, and storage
- Procedures for booth space applications, acceptance, and allocation policies for booth reservations
- Insurance requirements and "hold harmless" clauses
- Number of exhibitors allowed to attend vis à vis size of booth
- Registration procedures and credentialing
- Enforcement and sanction prerogatives of the sponsoring association

While this sounds more like a legal document than a marketing tool, it is the foundation for a solid exhibit sales effort. Through creative design and clear detail, the prospectus is the cornerstone on which the marketer builds the image of a professionally presented event. The fewer questions potential exhibitors have about the exposition, the fewer calls will be placed to the marketing office and the faster they will select their booths!

Incentives to Increase Sales

Strategies for increasing booth sales, and rewarding loyalty, are limited only by the marketing executive's imagination. There are some tried-and-true approaches routinely employed.

Exhibitors look for *exposure.* Line of sight from buyers to a

booth location is critical. A booth at the hall entrance is much preferred over a booth sandwiched in the middle of the aisle in a far
corner of the room. Typically, prices will reflect a premium charge
for greater exposure to traffic patterns. Everyone has seen the corner booth with the crowd gathered around the two-dimensional
line of sight, and then observed the less fortunate exhibitor in a
less exposed location, lamenting that "no one knows we're here!"
This is a common challenge.

Marketers should emphasize to potential exhibitors that the
best locations will sell out first. Floor plan designers should work
with the marketing team to provide premium price opportunities
and to promote to potential buyers an urgency to secure the best
booth locations before competitors sign the space contract. Among
those floor plan strategies that increase marketability and pricing
are these designs:

1. **"Island" Booths.** These are stand-alone booths with no immediate neighbors and with buyer sight lines available from
   all four directions. These are typically desired by larger exhibitors, seeking to maximize exposure at a higher price.
2. **Corner Booths.** Located on the corners of booth aisles, they
   offer line of sight from two directions.
3. **Hall Entry Booths.** Facing the hall entry points, these exhibitors have the first chance to attract buyers as they visit
   the exposition.
4. **Dining Area Booths.** Many expositions provide foodservice
   areas to keep buyers from leaving the hall at mealtime.
   Booths adjacent to dining areas are favored by many exhibitors because of the constant traffic promised by foodservice areas.
5. **"Bookstore" Booth Locations.** An increasingly popular exposition feature is the association's "bookstore," or an area
   in which attendees are encouraged to see and purchase organizational and industry publications. As with the dining
   areas, these features draw crowds and proximity to them is
   of benefit to exhibitors with this beneficial line of sight.

In addition, space rental discounts should be considered to reward loyalty for previous exhibitors. Early deadlines for choice locations are also a staple marketing to previous exhibitors, as well
as first-in-line booth selections for exhibitors, based on number of

years of participation, degree of participation, and sponsorship support.

The organization's most essential obligation is to put traffic in the exhibit aisles to fulfill exhibitor expectations and ensure repeat business. Marketing is a key to successful exposition management and growth as well as the substantial revenue it can drive. Adequate attention and budget must be devoted to promoting attendance and making participation convenient.

Full use should be made of industry publications, association journals, and print/electronic media to promote the importance of the exposition to attendees/buyers. Articles, ads, and interviews in print should continuously promote the exposition as a major component of the convention experience.

In many cases, exhibits must be located away from the conference facility because of a lack of space. In these instances, buses should be provided to make travel to the exhibits convenient for buyers (making certain the bus service is also available to exhibitors, who must be at the show earlier, and stay later, than their audiences). Without such service, it is too easy for buyers to stop by the restaurant or dawdle in the bar rather than walk or wait for taxis for transport to the trade show. Transportation is a small investment to fill the exhibit aisles, particularly in inclement weather.

Other methods of increasing floor traffic may include:

- Door prizes.
- Prize drawings (with the requirement that drawing stubs or business cards be deposited by attendees in exhibit booths in order to be eligible for the big prize). This involves exhibitors in the festivities, drives attendees toward the booths, and incrementally increases the exhibitors' number of "leads."
- Exhibit hours that are noncompetitive with other convention events such as seminars, leadership meetings, and food functions. This dedicated time for the exposition reflects the importance that the association attaches to its exposition.
- Celebrity "walk-arounds" or appearances on the show floor.
- Inviting exhibitors to give away prizes, samples, and even specialty snacks or dessert items from their booths to increase visits by buyers.
- Providing a photographer to take memento pictures for attendees to take home.

- Having live music and entertainment at the hall entrance to attract crowds and build excitement.

The marketer must be sensitive to the need to maintain balance between the number of booths sold and the attendance. Empty aisles will quickly override the temptation to oversell booths, because the exhibitors won't come back. Equally important is that too few exhibitors will frustrate a large crowd of buyers. That equation of balance is critical to incremental growth and long-term success. The true sign of marketing success will be the day when veteran exhibitors return to sign up for their booths, leaving a waiting list for those hoping to get on board and be a part of the profitable action.

Marketing Other Convention Events

The reasons for attending a convention are numerous and varied, depending on the priorities, interests, and tastes of the individuals being solicited. The marketing approach must reflect the interests of the members, their families, and guests. Association members will often base their reason to attend on the educational programs, seminars, and symposia (whether or not that is true). It is easier to sell the boss on the need to take time from work and spend money for continuing education than it is for parties and tours. Spouses, on the other hand, will more likely be drawn by social functions, entertainment, and seeing old friends. Elected association leaders are often seeking recognition and political opportunities. Children will be drawn by the youth program and the chance to make new friends. The incentives are often cross-related and variable. Marketing, through all the tools described earlier, should address every identifiable asset of the event program and emphasize more definitive and specific benefits to the greatest extent possible through market research and segmentation.

That research should include:

- **Analysis.** Finding a need and filling it
- **Communications.** Providing information and listening to reactions
- **Differentiation.** Distinguishing your offering from similar offerings and making it more compelling

- **Target Selection.** Identifying the markets most likely to buy
- **Valuation.** Matching the costs to perceived value
- **Vehicles.** Selecting the most effective channels of promotion

When marketing the educational benefits, emphasis should be placed on the credibility of presenters, in particular, their bios, academic and professional credentials and designations, and a capsule of the content to be presented. "This is what you will learn" is the benefit that must be carried in the message. Vague descriptions and bland session titles will not drive adequate response. Punch it up! Make it creative and compelling! A seminar can be a "career-changing opportunity." A symposium can be "an exciting exchange of ideas and concepts." A general session can be "the place where our association comes together to view the future." And a leadership, board of directors, or committee meeting can be "where we steer our association into the new millennium."

This may require separate marketing vehicles aimed at separate market segments. The issue of time-cost commitment to return on investment requires research and measurement of attendance results for each segment. Coding letters, brochures, coupons, and other response/registration forms will identify the respondent category and provide rich information on the effectiveness of the various marketing approaches used.

In the final analysis, the marketing investment should be designed to have "legs," in other words, to legitimately provide an experience that will be memorable for participants regardless of the market segments they represent. If their expectations are fulfilled, they will value their investment enough to invest again, bringing to one's mind the old sales adage: "The easiest sale is the repeat sale."

Summary

Associations present unique challenges for the event marketer, primarily because of the typical (and often conflicting) leadership boards and committees, the voluntary nature of the stakeholders, and the fact that the attendee market must be convinced of the value of investing time and money in the event. Therefore, market segmentation and research are of extreme importance. Continuous maintenance of lists is critical due to the mobile nature of the membership itself. Millions of dollars are wasted each year on printing, postage, and electronic communications as a result of outdated target information.

Beyond current lists, the marketing executive must be vigilant in the search for new audiences. Focus groups and other research can help identify related markets that could benefit from the event, and perhaps even be invited to join the organization on a permanent basis. Suppliers and exhibitors are often significant resources for lists of potential attendees, as well as for cross-promotions for the event. Regardless of the targets, the message must emphasize the *benefits* that the registrant can expect to receive, rather than the *features* of the event. From the advertising to the brochures to the public relations, the message must be constant, crisp, easy to understand, and compelling.

TALES FROM THE FRONT

An association of veteran business executives researched attendee needs for the convention program and learned an interesting thing from respondents. They were frustrated by limited time available for peer interchange and too much time spent passively in seminar rooms being lectured to by presenters and panels. The marketing approach was changed to reflect the true demographics and attitudes of the constituency. In other words, these were industry captains, accustomed to being heard and having their opinions weighed heavily.

In response, the marketer prevailed upon convention planners to allocate a two-hour period in which to provide "topic tables," or free-form discussion groups with prescribed industry issues to debate in an informal setting. The executives could flow from table to table and topic to topic and stay as long or as little as they liked at each. The convention staff was amazed at the sight. High-ranking executives had the room abuzz with conversation and were obviously enjoying the opportunity to grab a chair and a cup of coffee, rub elbows with peers, pontificate and debate, and make new business contacts and friends.

The reaction in postevent research was so positive that a full six hours of the "topic table" approach to education was built into the convention schedule. Follow-up has proved that this informal, inexpensive, and fulfilling educational format has become the leading reason cited by attendees for repeat attendance.

Chapter Challenge

1. You have been asked to develop an external marketing campaign in a community that has never before hosted your convention. What local resources would you pursue in that community to implement your campaign, and what marketing approaches would you attempt with each?

2. You have been given the responsibility for organizing an internal list management program for your direct-mail department. What tools and strategies would you use to ensure that your lists are correct and current, and what resources are available to augment the list with data on new potential members and attendees?

CHAPTER 6

Marketing Corporate Meetings, Products, Services, and Events

Selling the Company's Objectives

What We Have Here Is an Insurmountable Opportunity

—Yogi Berra

WHEN YOU HAVE COMPLETED THIS CHAPTER, YOU WILL BE ABLE TO:

- Translate the corporate message and mission into sales and marketing
- Market the spirit and purpose of incentive programs
- Understand the nuances between internal and external communications and markets
- Establish meaningful and durable relationships with the media
- Appreciate the role of public relations in corporate event marketing
- Understand the growing role of cause-related marketing in an overall corporate image-building campaign

---

Many in event marketing find themselves in a position to market both association and corporate events. Often, independent event and production companies provide marketing expertise for their clients, and it is common for nonprofit association marketing executives to make the transition to a for-profit corporation to promote their events and vice versa. Consequently, it is essential that you, as a marketer, innately understand the significant differences between the two "cultures" and profiles: nonprofit associations and societies (discussed in Chapter 5) and for-profit corporations. The differences from a marketing perspective may be subtle, but they are nonetheless significant. Understanding both will broaden your marketing skills to attract a broader scope of potential clients.

Many of the principles of event marketing are similar for association and corporate activities. But the markets to which those efforts are targeted are markedly different in many respects. These distinctions are fundamental to you as an event marketing professional with a broad appeal to both types of institutions.

Differences Between Corporate and Association Events

Corporate	**Association**
Most events are discretionary.	Most events are mandatory.
Decision making is centralized.	Decision making is decentralized.
Budget is fixed.	Budget is variable.
Attendance is mandatory.	Attendance is voluntary.
Function participation is mandatory.	Function participation is voluntary.
Purpose of attendance is consistent.	Purpose of attendance is variable.
Hotel "booking" lead times may be short.	Hotel "booking" lead times are longer.
Usually geographically unrestricted.	Often geographically restricted.

Defining the Differences

Most corporate meetings and events are discretionary; that is, they are subject to the decisions of management. For example, incentive trips and events may not be held if employees have fallen short of quotas, or if the company is performing below expectations. Recognition programs may not occur if management deems that there is no one worthy of the award. Product introduction spectaculars may or may not be held, depending on whether or not there are products innovative enough to herald their arrival with great fanfare before employees and buyers. The discretionary leverage of management to schedule an event, not schedule an event, or even cancel a scheduled one is paramount in most corporate meetings. The exception may be an annual shareholders' meeting required by corporate mandate.

On the other hand, if you are marketing association meetings, you will find the schedule much more mandatory and predictable. Association bylaws normally require an annual membership convention, perhaps two or three board and leadership meetings, and even a midyear leadership conference. Committees permeate associations, and they all meet. These events are normally held at similar times of the year and with somewhat constant attendance profiles. The point is that they are stipulated by organizational doctrine and are rarely canceled.

The sensitivity to economic conditions also varies between corporate and association events. In the economic decline in the United States during the 1980s, for example, the number of corporate events declined as well. Corporate profits were down, research and development for new products were curbed, and incentives for sales quotas were diminished. The market for corporate meetings is greatest in economic good times and reduced in times of recession. The terrorist attacks of September 11, 2001, and the resulting economic downturn are stark examples of the negative impact on the events industry.

Comparatively, association events often grow in number and scope when economic times are tough. The reason? Remember that corporations are "for-profit" entities: The bottom line means everything. But associations are "not-for-profit" institutions, where helping members solve problems is the preeminent reason for existing. People join associations to further their careers, improve their professional or business fortunes, and learn to survive economic and political misfortunes. In other words, there is comfort in the company of others when through association interaction one can find commiseration and empathetic colleagues in the face of threats. Therefore, it is not unusual to find greater marketing opportunities for association events in bad times than in good times in which the members don't feel so urgent a need to congregate, learn, and solve problems with peers. But the association marketing message is critical in driving home the theme that "help is on the way. Come take advantage of it."

Still another major difference between corporate and association events is the decision-making organizational structure. In the corporate sector, decisions are usually made by a president, a vice president of marketing, or a branch manager. Regardless, the decision is usually arbitrary, unimpeded by committee interaction and passed along as company doctrine to event planners and marketers. The decision making in an association environment is quite different. One event may be the subject of preferences and debate among many committees or councils, including the executive committee, the board of directors, the site selection committee, the education committee, the welcoming committee, the exposition committee, the spouse activities committee, and many more. Bear in mind that most of these volunteer leaders have little or no experience in event management and marketing. Even for the uninitiated, with associations the potential for confusion in direction, and delay in implementation, is obvious. If you are responsible for marketing the event, your clear tasks may become much more difficult to determine even as deadlines become tighter.

Budgetary considerations also vary greatly between corporate and association events. Corporations typically develop a preset budget for events, based on overall company projections and perceived value of the event itself. No registration income is anticipated because employees attend as part of their employers' requirements. Expense budgets are based on the overall financial operating plan and are static (unless a crisis strikes the corporation, which could affect not just the budget, but the validity of the event itself). Association budgets are highly varied and adjusted through time as income and expense factors change. Remembering that attendance is voluntary and less predictable, associations will monitor registration income carefully and adjust expenses up or down, depending on whether or not revenue will either create income over expense or at least cover expenses, as the overall association budget may require. Why is this of any importance to you as the marketing executive? Because when registration fees are falling short of expectations, additional registration revenue must be generated. In addition, other revenue may be increased to compensate for the shortfall. This could include sponsorships, exhibit fees, advertising income, and "services-in-kind" agreements with suppliers. All these efforts should be under the direction of the marketer and should be coordinated to fulfill the financial commitment the association staff has made to its board of directors. If a convention, for example, loses money, the association staff may be highly criticized for using dues and other funds to make up the difference and pay the convention bills. The effect of this is that monies intended for other purposes are being used to subsidize an event that not every dues-paying member can attend. The political issues are obvious.

Attendance provides still another stark contrast between most corporate and association events, and one that is simple to understand. When a corporation has a new product sales conference, for example, the sales staff is told to be there. The marketing effort here is to convey the message and purpose of the event, but not to encourage attendance. The boss will do that.

Attendance at association meetings is as voluntary as the invitees themselves. They will decide whether to spend the time and money to attend. No one can force them to come. As a result, the marketing team's primary responsibility is to use all the marketing disciplines described throughout this text to generate attendance and participation in all the event's components. Without attendance by an enthusiastic, excited audience, the quality of the event itself becomes academic.

The same can be said of the events' functions themselves. In the case of corporate meetings, participants are generally required to show up at all events. It is not unusual for the company to monitor employee attendance at seminars, new product introductions and descriptions, or sales meetings and discussion groups. They attend as part of their job responsibilities. Therefore, function participation is mandatory by the nature of official corporate meeting components. The attendees are being paid to attend, just as they are paid to be in their offices on certain days. This means that rooms will be full, guarantees will be precise and achieved, budgets will be accurately estimated, and the schedule tightly controlled.

Associations are voluntary. Their attendees are paying a registration fee to attend and can essentially participate in event functions to as little or great a degree as they wish. Food and beverage guarantees will carry much more guess work (and a great deal more financial risk). Similarly, one seminar room may be over-flowing, while another has barely drawn a dozen people. A dread of association event planners is to have a sparse audience for a key speaker, or a half-filled room with empty tables at the closing gala. It is the role of marketers to work with planners in scheduling events effectively and to project through the promotional arsenal at their command the magnetism and value each function holds for those who are attending the event.

As the marketing executive, you must also be sensitive to the purpose of attendance by your audience. For the corporate marketer, the purpose of attendance is relatively consistent. If the company calls its technical directors to a conference to learn about new concepts in broadband communications systems, their purpose for attending is relatively easy to define. You will want to develop a marketing approach that will clearly set forth the profile of the program, the expectations of attendee performance, and the positive results that they should anticipate.

Association event attendees' purposes for attending are much more difficult to homogenize. Why do they attend? Their emotions and aspirations may be disparate. The reasons may include any combination of a virtually endless list, some of which are shown in Figure 6-1. Through the research we have discussed earlier, the marketer must determine at best the criteria for attendance and the expectations of the audience in order to develop a market strategy that appeals to the majority of the association's members and guests.

It becomes clear that the corporate market could be described as homogeneous, while the typical association market is heterogeneous, in terms of purpose, individual priorities, and event expectations.

A few other comparisons are important to consider. For example, in "booking" or scheduling events, corporate meetings and conferences are known for relatively short lead times for organizing many events. Because of the more predictable and established timing of mandated association events and the need to promote attendance, associations are known for longer lead times. If you are marketing the corporate event, this means that you may be working with a much tighter timeline than your association counterpart to strategize, develop, and deliver a marketing plan that achieves the company's objectives prior to the event date. Association

- Attend educational programs
- Network
- Pursue political ambition
- Solve a personal or business problem
- See new exhibitor products/services
- Go to parties
- See a unique venue or city
- Hear a famous speaker or see a celebrity entertainer
- Investigate a new industry/profession
- Participate in sports and recreation
- Just "get away from home"

Figure 6-1
Motivation to attend for the association participant typically is more inconsistent, variable, and overlapping than that of the corporate event attendee. The degree to which attendance is voluntary (association) or mandatory (corporation) will affect the marketer's message significantly.

marketers typically have a longer lead time, allowing a well-considered critical-path approach to promotion, public relations, and communications strategies. And, in most cases, they will have more time to make marketing strategy adjustments as variable response levels may require.

Here are a few more brief, but important tips for you to remember when marketing either a corporate or an association event:

- In the corporate event world, the market is composed of one affiliation: the company being marketed. Its corporate culture, ideals, issues, and operational philosophies are relatively consistent throughout its employee family. They all salute the same flag. In marketing their events, you will want to identify those corporate characteristics clearly before establishing a marketing strategy.
- Typically in the association event world, the market is composed of a myriad of cultures, issues, and ideals. You must remember that while a trade association represents a specific industry (e.g., agriculture, transportation, or paper manufacturing), its members are owners and operators of perhaps thousands of individual businesses. Many of them may even compete against one another. They join the association for many reasons, the most basic of which is to improve their businesses in order to compete more effectively and be profitable, or at least solvent. Therefore, while the association that serves them is considered altruistic and nonprofit, the

motivations of its audience likely will be driven by improving their individual profits, education, and competitiveness. This heterogeneous and complex mix of priorities within the association market presents a daunting challenge for you to identify and sell the *benefits* (before you sell the *features*) of the event. This is yet another argument for effective quantitative and qualitative market research.

- Corporations can usually take their events anywhere they want. Incentive trips will usually be booked in exotic locations and resorts, the most popular of which are in Hawaii and Florida. As companies participate increasingly in the global market, more than ever events such as product introductions and sales blitzes are held throughout the world. For marketing, this means that the promotional emphasis may stress the location as well as the purpose of the event itself.

- On the other hand, associations may be restricted by covenant or bylaws to certain areas. A state or county educational association may not be permitted to convene outside of its home locale. A national society in the United States may be restricted to a U.S. venue for certain events. An adroit marketer will determine this before preparing a marketing proposal that, because of this lack of understanding, may be considered invalid at the outset by the sponsoring organization.

Now that you understand the critical differences between association and corporate communities as target markets, let us turn our attention solely to the corporate market.

Selling the Corporate Message

To sell the corporate message, you need to understand the corporate culture of your client or employer. *Webster's Unabridged Dictionary* defines *culture* as "the integrated pattern of human behavior that includes thought, speech, action, and artifacts and depends upon man's capacity for learning and transmitting knowledge to succeeding generations." In addition, it cites "the customary beliefs, social forms, and material traits of a racial, religious, or social group." To that definition, we could add "or corporation."

Employees are imbued with the ideals, slogans, and symbols of the company. Events will often personify these through speeches, audiovisual productions, flags and banners, and even songs and rituals that stir the spirit and reinforce the corporate message. For instance, a highlight of events produced by Mary Kay Cosmetics, Inc., is the moment when its distributors stand en masse and sing the corporate theme song "I've Got the Mary Kay Spirit Down in My Heart!" with such enthusiasm that passersby stop and watch through the ballroom doors.

The corporate culture engenders the corporate message to both its employees and its customers. Older, more established companies such as Xerox and IBM are known for their dress codes and uniform approach to sales and service. While their regimentation has been relaxed somewhat in recent years as younger generations enter their workforces and markets, the image of a strong business focus remains embedded in their cultures and the perception of their clients. By contrast, the more newly arrived Silicon Valley and dot-com genre of companies embraces casual dress and a work-hard, play-hard philosophy. Employees are encouraged to take time out for exercise, to stroll through the office park, to participate in family days, and even to bring their dogs to work.

Understanding the underpinnings of a corporation's behavioral expectations is essential in marketing its events. Management and decision makers will help you understand not just the nature of the culture, but also the *reasons* for which that culture exists. Is it to attract a certain type of employee persona? Is it to attract a certain generation of market segments? If you are marketing that corporate message to its employees, shareholders, customers, and allies, ask decision makers the following types of questions:

- Where did the company come from? How long has it existed? Where does it expect to go (short- and long-range projections)?
- What has worked? What has not?
- What is the corporate working environment? A casual "dress down" company executive will likely welcome a casual "warm and fuzzy" approach. The converse will probably be true with a more tradition-oriented enterprise.
- Who are the major competitors? How do their values and corporate philosophies differ? What makes us better (what should be emphasized)? What makes us worse (what must we correct)?
- Who are the corporate heroes, past and present? How can we honor them to set standards of performance for our employees who gather at the event?

- Are there any traditions or rituals that must be presented to project the corporate message, such as company songs and slogans, festivals, contests, sports and recreation activities, and family-oriented activities?
- What adjustments or evolutionary changes in the corporate message are desired, to be introduced at the event but, even more important, to be projected through the marketing strategy that precedes the event and establishes the desired message?
- Is there a formal set of policies and procedures establishing corporate behavior? Elements such as internal standards of addressing other employees of different rank and other interactions, decorum for public behavior, and requirements for meeting preparation and participation are essential to understanding the profile of the company and the expectation of its employees.

It is essential that you *do your homework*. The diversity of corporate cultures and messages are complex and wide. Applying one set of marketing strategies to one company's needs will not apply to all. The successful marketing executive reads the needs of the corporation before prescribing the marketing plan.

Marketing Incentive Programs

Incentive programs are designed with one element in mind: to reward exceptional sales performance and other levels of achievement by employees during a defined period of time, in order to meet corporate goals and objectives. Standards to be achieved for an employee to become eligible often include sales, but also may involve production levels, tenure with the company, new ideas and concepts, or cost-saving strategies.

More than any other type of corporate event, the incentive program demands that effective marketing be utilized from the beginning to emphasize the levels of performance required to win a trip to an exotic location (often with spouse or guest) or a special award or bonus. Extensive promotion should begin at the time the goals of the company and the rewards available for achieving those goals are established. It should continue throughout the campaign to keep those targets in front of employees and remind them of the deadlines toward which they are working to be eligible for that odyssey to the South of France or that "Employee of the Year" award with a generous bonus.

Typically, incentive programs involve an all-expenses-paid vacation to lavish resort properties or overseas destinations and are proven strategies in fulfilling corporate goals and objectives. They differ from other corporate events in that the primary reason for holding them is fun, not work. Nevertheless, a portion of the itinerary will often be devoted to workshops or general sessions, and should be promoted as such in the corporation's internal advertising and direct-mail pieces. But, in most cases, and unlike most other corporate events, these "working" sessions are not compulsory for attendees and are short in duration (or canceled entirely). The printed program, however, may allow the participant to avoid reporting the value of the trip as taxable income. Other companies will hold meaningful business sessions during incentive trips, primarily to announce industry innovations or new products and reestablish the corporate culture and employee loyalty. An incentive group on board a cruise ship, for example, offers a tempting "captive audience" for management. When you are marketing an incentive program, be certain to understand the real intentions of management in the program mix in order to establish your promotional priorities.

Remember these basics of marketing incentive programs. They are simple, but critical points of emphasis as described in Figure 6-2.

- Use incentive programs to motivate employees.
- Describe in glowing terms the rewards and venues/destinations.
- Emphasize the monetary value of the prize or trip.
- Clearly prescribe the levels of achievement necessary.
- Identify timelines and deadlines.
- Always remind employees where the benefits are coming from. The *corporation* is rewarding its own for good work, well done (and creating employee loyalty)!

Figure 6-2
Clearly defining the rules and expectations for a corporate incentive event is a major responsibility of marketing. Building excitement must be blended with defining the responsibilities required of all participants.

Other Types of Corporate Meetings

There are numerous purposes for which corporate events are planned, many of which incorporate the same marketing principles described earlier. Among them are:

1. **Training Seminars.** Similar to association seminars and workshops, these sessions incorporate speakers and panels discussing specific subjects such as industry trends, new scientific discoveries and theories, and changing market demographics. A clear concept of the topic and the benefit *(what the participant will learn)* is an important goal of marketing the message to participants.
2. **Product Introductions.** New product introductions are multipurpose events. They are primarily educational events, designed to teach salespeople and corporate officials the benefits of new products or services they must sell. In addition, the gathering may be used for ancillary management meetings or franchise orientation sessions. Product introductions may also feature *celebrations* of new products and corporate innovations, aimed at corporate employees as well as wholesalers, distributors, retailers, and even the general public. Dramatic presentations, complete with cutting-edge audiovisual extravaganzas, elaborate staging, music, and entertainment, are often the platform upon which new products are displayed and described.

What does this mean to those who market such events? Obviously, the nature and level of sophistication of the event will bear on the marketing approach. The key, however, is this: An analogy can be made to the difference between corporate and association meetings regarding mandated versus voluntary attendance. A new product introduction for company employees mandates their attendance. The *message* must be promoted, but not the attendance. However, distributors and wholesalers are typically less subject to corporate requirements for attendance. They are often more independent from the corporation in the distribution and delivery systems and, in those cases, must be persuaded to attend through marketing. This is truer for retailers, who sell many brands and products and may be less interested in learning firsthand the details of the new products. For those publics desired to be in attendance, the market segments for promotion may include general publics reached through advertising, radio and television commercials, requests for coverage by the print and electronic media, and bus, subway, and other transit signage. These marketing tools are often used for auto shows, boat shows, and flower shows aimed at the general public. However, the target market may be as specific as government agencies, former and present clients, or public health officials. A clear understanding of the corporation's desired audience is critical to developing a responsive marketing plan.

1. **Management Meetings.** Often a mixture of executive-level interaction, symposia, and recreation, these events may require little marketing because attendance is a badge of achievement in the corporation. Still, a major part of the educational content may be intensive discussions of corporate philosophies and values, problem solving, and new organizational strategies. Advance information should prepare participants for the challenges and anticipated results of those discussions so that contributions by attendees will be maximized.

2. **Sales Meetings.** From a marketing perspective, national and regional sales meetings usually combine the promotional approaches required for both educational and training events and those for product introductions. The purposes blend the sharpening of sales skills, the reinforcing of corporate values and philosophies, and the learning of new features of products and services to be sold. These are typically work/play events, designed first to educate and then to recreate and entertain, in order to bolster enthusiasm and send the salesforce home with new dedication to moving the product to the consumer.

3. **Stockholders' Meetings.** Stockholders are major "stakeholders" in the corporation. Corporate constitutions and laws usually require at least one meeting of stockholders per year. These meetings are held to apprise stockholders of corporate success, or lack of it, and to invite stockholders to ask questions, offer advice, or just complain to company management. They may be highly celebratory in good times or deeply adversarial in bad times. The format of these meetings, and the degree to which they are promoted, is a highly

sensitive management issue. It behooves the marketing executive to carefully follow the directions of management in developing a marketing approach, if any is required at all.

Internal and External Communications

Whether the corporate event is the grand opening of a new shopping mall, introducing an upcoming auto show, or cutting a ribbon for a new dealership, both internal and external communications should be strategized.

Communicating the corporate event is most effective when both internal and external resources are embraced. For example, the purposes of a training program should be communicated first through appropriate channels within the headquarters office. Focus group reaction may be invited and adjustments made to the program, prior to dissemination of the information to branch offices, distributor regions, retailers, or other markets to persuade them to attend the event.

The typical internal departments that should be considered for the focus group may include:

- Executive management
- Public relations
- Marketing
- Human resources
- Corporate events
- Sales
- Franchisee, distributor, and wholesaler divisions
- Finance
- New product
- Research and development

Not unlike a product launch, the marketer should consider this an "idea launch" in order to invite candid response and facilitate fine-tuning before turning to external communications to create awareness and enthusiasm for the event. Further, the exercise will create a proprietary interest in the enterprise among those throughout the corporate headquarters, whose support is essential for the success of the project.

When refined through internal input, the event program can be introduced through traditional marketing forces such as public relations, advertising, specialty advertising items, e-mail, the Internet, and press kits to begin the external communications process.

With corporate meetings, internal communications are essential in delivering the message, creating an understanding of the message of the event and the corporate posture for its intended achievement. Attendance is not the purpose of the internal communication, but enthusiasm for the purpose of attending is. The external communications effort will be more expansive and expensive, but worth the effort if market research has been thorough. As we have noted earlier, distributors, franchise owners, retailers, and other external markets such as the general public may have to be attracted and persuaded to attend. Whether attracting local awareness to the corporation's presence or trumpeting the opening of a new shopping mall or public park, external communications may include a number of marketing elements and "mini-events" designed to attract attention. The communication should be designed not just to create awareness and interest, but also to sustain an increasing excitement that will build until the opening curtain.

Some tools for external communications are worth further consideration:

- Press releases and press kits
- Street fairs, parades, and stunts
- Sample products and descriptive literature
- Street banners, outdoor advertising, and transit system posters
- Public relations campaigns aimed at local officials
- Book signings and celebrity appearances
- Special discounts offered by participating merchants
- Press conferences
- Receptions for local leaders and corporate executives
- Public service announcements (PSAs)
- Requests for coverage (print and electronic media)

Each corporate event, regardless of its nature, is primarily designed to serve the interests, goals, and objectives of the company. Internal communications are aimed at the targeted employees of the firm. External communications are aimed at customers, suppliers, stockholders, distributors, wholesalers, retailers, and others (such as the general public) who are not under the direct control of the corporation, but are critical to its marketing successes.

Maximizing Media Relationships

If you are responsible for marketing a corporate event, your greatest challenge may be to impress upon media of all types that the event is "newsworthy" and of importance in providing benefits for those interested in the product or service. To achieve this, the marketing professional will identify the elements of the event that will have a positive impact on the community at large: A unique product introduction; a community service; financial contributions to, or corporate investment in, a city asset are among the approaches that will grab the attention of local print and electronic media. On the other hand, simply issuing a press release that your company is holding its national sales meeting at the local convention center probably will not raise the eyebrows of the news editor. While advertising is an effective media tool, it is inherently considered biased. Nothing establishes credibility as well as editorial coverage of the event and its purpose.

The marketing approach requires research into the media options within any geographic area being targeted. There exist numerous media alternatives in which awareness, and even personal relationships, may be established and reinforced.

Print Media

- Trade publications
- Industry and consumer magazines and periodicals
- Internal and external newsletters
- Newspapers
- Local/county shopping news
- Business journals
- Church bulletins
- Flyers for office reception areas and customer counters
- Publications of allied companies and related associations
- Publications of schools and colleges
- Travel and airline publications

Electronic Media

- Radio
- Television
- Internet
- Cable
- Broadcast fax

A careful analysis of the markets reached by each of the media is necessary. The larger events may target national newspapers and television/radio outlets with broad demographics. Smaller corporate meeting marketers will seek relationships with state or county newspapers, regional or local broadcasters, local shopping guides, and merchants who may hold an interest in the purpose or products of the corporation. The issue of a universal shotgun approach versus a tightly segmented media reach should be based on the nature of the event, the benefits that can legitimately be explained to the targeted market segment, and the economic viability and costs of the promotion itself.

Often, establishing media relationships requires personal intervention. City editors and news desks receive bundles of press releases and product announcements, a burdensome mountain of materials to review each day. It is too easy for your pronouncement to get buried in the pile.

There are some strategies that will help in establishing media relationships that can be personal and enduring:

1. Find an ally who can facilitate the right contacts. Think for a minute. Which franchisee in the target market is a "mover and shaker" in the community? Which distributor serves on the city council and knows those who influence attitudes? Who is capable of carrying the flag locally, providing the marketing department with inside advice and paving the way to new media relationships? Media relationships may begin with allies and supporters not necessarily directly connected with media outlets themselves. In this case, it is not what you know, it is whom you know.

2. Determine the message and match it with the medium that will be interested in that message. A newspaper's executive editor may or may not be caught by your message. A television producer may or may not pass on your press release

to the right desk. The message should be targeted as precisely as possible to the party most interested. For example, if your message is:

- Finance: financial editor/finance desk
- Sports/recreation: sports editor
- Fashions: style section, fashion editor
- Business: business editor/consumer news
- Food: food section editor
- Entertainment: entertainment section/reviewers

In other words, the more specifically the target may be sighted, the more enhanced will be the chance that the communication will be greeted by a receptive media representative. With this in mind, your allies and supporters in the market locale (discussed in item 1 above) may help you in making the right contact at the right time. Ask for and get permission to use their names as references.

1. Send a personal letter, perhaps with a press release, to the proper media contacts, illustrating the mission and the message of the corporate event, and alert them that you will be calling to offer additional information and answer questions. This further creates awareness and is a considerate business practice. A "cold call" often is not an effective method of establishing a relationship with media representatives unless your message is truly "hot" and of community interest. If the message is sufficiently compelling, the marketer will often get an uninitiated phone call from the news editor or a reporter assigned to follow up on the story.
2. Maintain the contacts after the coverage. If the event is reported on the local newscast, or coverage has appeared in the print media, or local merchants and franchisees have distributed materials and posted signage in their windows, let them know the importance of this to the corporation. While they may not be marketing targets at future events, they probably know people who are. They may well become additional allies in the effort to key media players and maximize new relationships.

The marketer will be practicing the impersonal disciplines of the profession, such as analyzing the costs of urban/suburban coverage, the validity of discounts and coupons, and return on investment for the campaign. Nevertheless, he or she must never forget that establishing and maximizing relationships with the media implies considerate and continuing interaction with *people*. Personal and peer recognition, whether it is a professional letter or a birthday card, is priceless.

Public Relations Opportunities

The value and practice of effective public relations in marketing corporate events has been discussed extensively throughout this text. The principles do not change substantially among the promotional strategies for corporate, association, labor, social, or community events. The key point is that the value of public relations is based on what people *say about your corporation,* rather than what the corporation *says about itself*. The gain in credibility among the customer universe is obvious. The financial value of effective public relations is equally important. The Public Relations Society of America, the largest organization of public relations professionals in the United States, estimates that the positive financial impact of editorial coverage of an event is three times that of an advertisement by the sponsoring company.

Like its association event counterparts, the corporate public relations strategies should employ quantitative and qualitative research, focus groups, interviews, attitude surveys, and lifestyle/demographic analysis in planning and implementing the campaign.

Cause-Related Events

As a public relations tool, these events have become a staple in positioning corporations as community-oriented entities, sensitive to their role in assisting efforts to promote the common cause. Whether employed as an ancillary feature of a corporate sales meeting or product introduction event, or as a stand-alone production, corporate sponsorship of an activity designed to call attention to a public need helps to establish the sponsoring company as a sensitive contributor within the country or the community. Raising money for a charity or an educational foundation for a target market association positions that corporation not just as a seller of products to their constituents, but also as a partner in the more altruistic purposes embraced by the target audience. In a public relations sense, few opportunities exceed cause-related marketing in gaining access to the press, community leaders, churches, charities, and the person in the street.

Ideas for corporate cause-related events are infinite, among them:

- Sponsorship of an AIDS Run or Race for the Cure™
- Sponsorship of a silent auction/reception to raise funds for a local Boys Club or Girls Club
- Sponsorship of a "Sports Day" for inner-city children
- Sponsorship of a cleanup campaign for a community park
- Sponsorship of a recognition day and festival to honor the police department and firefighters
- Sponsorship of a Thanksgiving fundraiser to help feed the homeless and indigent
- Sponsorship of a program designed to raise funds for schoolbooks and teaching aids

Cause-related programs are fertile fields in which to develop cross-promotions with others. Related companies, associations, community groups, and religious organizations may welcome the opportunity to join the effort. This can measurably increase the impact and acceptance of the cause, as well as the response of the target markets being invited to participate.

Additionally, cause-related promotions are an effective public relations tool in softening attitudes toward a corporation that may be attempting to overcome negative public opinion. Tobacco companies are an example of such an industry. The Philip Morris Companies produces many food products unrelated to its more recognized tobacco products. With sensitivity to the debate and negative public image of the tobacco industry, Philip Morris ran national television advertisements illustrating its airlifting of foods and other products to aid the war-ravaged people of Kosovo. It was an effective campaign that not only positioned the company as humanitarian and community spirited, but also illustrated the breadth of its product line. Such cause-related campaigns may be global or local in scope. But they are almost guaranteed to gain positive public relations value and corporate recognition.

Summary

Many in event marketing serve both corporate and association clients or employers during their careers. Therefore, the need for understanding the significant differences between the two is vital. This chapter has explored in detail many of those glaring, and sometimes subtle, differences. For corporation events, the corporate culture, its values, and its strategies for the future are paramount to successfully delivering the marketing message. A thorough investigation of the past history of the firm, and the results of its past events, is essential to understanding its aims for the future.

Corporations are centralized in decision-making authority. Therefore, understanding the mission and gaining approval for the marketing strategies are typically simplified. Budget considerations are usually relatively fixed, taking much of the guesswork out of the resources available for the marketing effort. However, as this chapter has demonstrated, the allocation of those resources to internal and external communications in the proper ratio will be an underlying qualifier for the success of the marketing campaign. Finally, because corporations are for-profit companies and often viewed by the media as somewhat biased toward company goals, the establishment of continuing and personal media relationships is a unique challenge, and opportunity, for the marketing executive.

TALES FROM THE FRONT

The Bowie (Maryland) Baysox is a minor league baseball team, one of the member teams within the Baltimore Orioles farm system. In July 2001, the city of Baltimore was paralyzed by a train derailment and consequent fire in a tunnel adjacent to Oriole Park at Camden Yards, the home stadium of the Orioles and the location for a long home stand of major league baseball. With the tunnel ablaze and toxic smoke pouring into that area of the city, all Oriole games had to be canceled for four days. City fire and police officials could not endanger the health of 45,000 fans and solve the traffic problems that the congestion would create with many roads closed by the accident.

The Bowie Baysox public relations department responded with a unique public service and promotional strategy. Through television and radio news reports, as well as regional advertising, the minor league team (whose stadium is an accessible 20 miles from Baltimore) invited disappointed fans whose Oriole games were canceled to bring their Oriole tickets to a Baysox game. Upon showing the ticket, the fans could buy a ticket to that Baysox game, have their Oriole ticket returned to them for use at the Orioles' makeup games, and also receive a free ticket to a future Baysox game. What was accomplished with that marketing strategy? The minor league team created a unique form of cross-promotion, a sense of community spirit, bigger crowds, and happy fans. In addition, the Baysox generated a new customer awareness of the team, its convenient location, and the charm of small-town minor league baseball in its market area.

Chapter Challenge

1. You have been asked to propose a promotional campaign for a corporation's annual sales conference and awards dinner. You have never worked in this capacity for this company in the past. What elements of the corporate culture would be important for you to know in analyzing the firm, its people, and its mission prior to preparing your proposal?

2. What steps would you take to establish relationships among the media in a community hosting the sales conference and awards dinner? How would you determine which components of the media should be included?

CHAPTER 7

Marketing Festivals, Fairs, and Other Special Events

Experience Is the Name Everyone Gives to Their Mistakes

—OSCAR WILDE

WHEN YOU HAVE COMPLETED THIS CHAPTER, YOU WILL BE ABLE TO:

- Create a marketing program unique to festivals, fairs, and other special events
- Coordinate sponsors and media programs
- Combine advertising, public relations, and promotions for special events
- Use street promotions and other unique methods to gain exposure
- Use celebrities and VIPs effectively
- Brand events for exclusive exposure
- Measure the effectiveness of marketing festivals and events
- Create guerrilla-marketing events

Marketing Festivals and Fairs

Today's festivals and fairs are more varied and sophisticated than ever before. Marketing these unique types of events requires unique and innovative tactics. In other words, the success of an event may not depend on the type of event, the star attraction, or the cause of the event, but on how well a marketer takes advantage of certain factors of the event. These factors include location, competition, weather, cost, and entertainment.

LOCATION

The selection and marketing of the location has a significant impact on attendance and the resulting success of an event. Is it centrally located or in a distant suburb? Is there easy road access from interstate highways or is there a subway stop within walking distance? Promoting easy access, a central location, or a new venue can contribute to greater attendance at your event. In addition, marketing the convenience of the location can increase acceptance of the event, and combining the historic or resort attributes can excite the potential attendees.

For years, the Baltimore Orioles baseball team played its home games at Memorial Stadium, an outdated stadium located in a rough neighborhood. When a new stadium was built in the rejuvenated Inner Harbor area of Baltimore and was designed to look like the ballfields of yesteryear, the stadium and its location became a bigger attraction than the team itself. The team sold out most of its home games the first year not because of a winning team, but because of the buzz created by the new stadium and its location. In the promotional messaging the ballclub used in selling tickets, one of the key marketing messages was for Oriole fans and nonfans to come out and visit this new masterpiece. The location was such a success that other Major League Baseball teams such as the Cleveland Indians and Texas Rangers copied the Orioles' marketing strategy with the same success.

COMPETITION

Promoting your event as unique, different, and better than the competitors' can be as important as the event itself. A marketer needs to advertise and promote the advantages of the event by showcasing the interesting and unique features. This requires a fully prepared marketing strategy. Sometimes using a marketing strategy in which you point out your differences can be effective, but there is also a risk in doing so. To name the competition can only give these competitors credibility and recognition. Unlike consumer products, such as the brand Suave, which advertises the fact that it is of the same quality as other brand names, but costs less, it is hard to use this as a marketing advantage in events. Traveling carnivals may promote the fact that they are a better value than a full-blown amusement park. However, it becomes evident to the consumer that $25 million of investment in rides and attractions may be a better experience.

When an event is successful, there can, and will be, imitators who market their events the same way, copying advertisements and themes as well as the look of the events. This can not only add to confusion for the public, but also hurt both the original event and the imitator in the end. Lollapalooza, a summer concert tour featuring a very diverse assortment of musical rock groups attracting fans in their teens and twenties, became a surprise runaway success in the concert business, breaking attendance records across the United States. After the second year of the tour, there were countless imitators marketing their tours in similar fashions, eventually giving music fans comparable choices.

WEATHER

Unlike a consumer product that is marketed on its own virtue, the weather can be an advantage or disadvantage in selling a special event. Weather can set the mood for the participants or consumers of the events. For example, consumer ski and travel shows typically take place in early November, a time that enables attendees to preview the latest ski equipment and ski resorts. Research has shown that, when the weather was cold, the show's attendance increased measurably. On the other hand, when the weather was unseasonably warm during the show, attendance declined dramatically. In these cases, the weather had a significant effect on the outcome of the event.

Weather also plays a big role in sporting events. Opening day of Major League Baseball is a unique event in which fans come outside to enjoy the end of winter and the beginning of spring. Professional beach volleyball's success has to do, in part, with the fact that the competitions take place in warm-weather areas where spectators can feel comfortable attending in a bathing suit or shorts to watch volleyball, complete with sand that is sometimes brought in to re-create a summer beach scene.

Indoor shows or events can be adversely affected if the weather is ideal. However, when the weather turns undesirable, it can keep people from outdoor leisure activities and bring them indoors to special events. A sophisticated marketer will be ready in these situations with advertisements on standby. When rain is forecast, the marketer will run local radio or TV advertisements promoting the public to come indoors in the wet weather.

There are hundreds of arts-and-crafts shows that are held in outdoor locations with exhibitors under portable pop-up tents. The success of these events depends on good weather, but everyone participates in these events with this understanding. One way marketers can ensure their success in promoting events that can be affected by the weather is to presell as many tickets as possible, sometimes at a deep discount, to guarantee attendance at these events. At the Vintage Virginia Wine Festival, tickets at a discount are sold in advance to guarantee substantial attendance. Part of the allure of the Super Bowl is that the event takes place in the middle of the winter in a warm climate or at an indoor venue. The success of marketing a golf tournament is better in May than in November. The success in selling concerts under the stars at outdoor amphitheaters has created a national summer concert season at amphitheaters, both new and old, across the country.

COST

The word "free" is used in fair, festival, and other special event advertisements because it attracts attention. If the cost is set at an attractive level, it needs to be included in the advertising. Cost and price can also be determining factors in marketing events as discussed in Chapter 4. When advertising a show, a marketer wants to be able to attract as wide an audience as possible to the event. For this reason, some events and shows that sell front-row seats at a premium do not even list the price of these tickets in advertisements but instead say "special seating available."

Sometimes a strategy with a high price can be successful when the event is positioned as something special. At other times, a value price that a larger, broader market can afford would be more successful.

The use of coupons can also make an event more attractive. When planning an event, the marketer generally tries to find a retail partner that can distribute discount coupons to attract a larger audience. Typically, retailers that feature these discount coupons are supermarket chains, drug stores, fast-food restaurants, and even pizza delivery chains. Another important source of discount coupons is in print advertising. By tagging a coupon in a print advertisement, there is the inclination for the public to tear out the advertisement, thus adding another reminder about the upcoming event.

ENTERTAINMENT

The success of an event is also dependent on the marketing of the entertainment. There are many types of entertainment that can be marketed in a variety of ways. For big-name stars, an interview on a radio station and a press release announcing tickets going on sale are effective for a quick sellout. Different and new types of entertainment, on the other hand, may require larger marketing and public relations budgets.

When "Defending the Caveman," a one-man comedy show, started playing in Washington, DC, there was a need for numerous newspaper advertisements and a public relations campaign to promote this alternative to the typical comedy club show. At the onset of the show, there had never been a truly successful one-man comedy show outside of Broadway. After the show ran in five cities and began to receive strong public relations support and word of mouth, it began selling out across the country, leading to Broadway's longest running comedy show. As the show moved from San Francisco to Dallas to Washington, the marketing was altered and became more sophisticated. What started with newspaper advertisements eventually moved to radio and direct mail.

Determining Appropriate Media for an Event

Certain types of media help elevate the excitement of events. For visual events, the marketer looks to use television advertisements. When print advertisements are desired, the use of color can lead to extra attention. Radio advertisements can set a mood or a theme and attract attention.

Cirque du Soleil, a new-wave, rock-and-roll Canadian circus, is difficult to describe. By the use of colorful print advertisements, however, prospective spectators can gain a sense of this type of event. Radio is very important for marketing musical events as sound is the key to these types of programs.

If you are marketing the annual home and garden show, do not randomly run advertisements in a local newspaper. Instead, target media that have a connection to the event. In the newspaper, target the weekly home or garden section. On radio, promote the event on the Saturday morning garden shows. On television, target cable TV networks like the Home and Garden network and shows like *This Old House.* By spending advertising dollars on media that relate directly to the product, you are being efficient with your media dollars. The marketer must look at the event and find the advertising opportunities that fit the event the best.

DEVELOPING A MARKETING SCHEDULE

The promotion of festivals, fairs, and concerts requires a different time schedule than other types of events. In promoting first-time events, one needs to educate the public to promote the new event. First-time events need to cut through the clutter. The consumer needs to be exposed to many different media, ranging from radio advertisements that heighten interest, to TV advertisements that visualize and excite, to print advertisements that give information, to Web sites that provide a comprehensive overview. In contrast, having a big-name band or movie star at an event will certainly contribute to its success, but needs to be promoted in a different way. There is a seesaw effect in scheduling a proper marketing program for this type of event.

You may want to allow extra time to promote the event. If promotions start too far out, however, it will be difficult to get the market to focus on the event. If promotions start too close to the event, there will not be enough time to educate the audience about your event. Let's look at two similar events with different histories.

Cirque du Soleil, the Canadian circus, has been touring in North America since 1984 and has built up a huge following. When this attraction comes to town, there is much more demand for tickets than supply of seats; thus, Cirque's promoters put tickets on sale over six months before the show comes to town. This strategy is successful as most shows sell out months in advance.

Barnum's Kaleidoscope, a similar circus attraction that premiered in 1999, had no history and had to resort to a larger marketing effort. This show's sales were more dependent on word of mouth and reviews after the shows had begun. More marketing efforts were undertaken during the entire run of the show, trying to build on the success of the earlier shows. If the run were successful, eventually Barnum's Kaleidoscope would be able to mimic Cirque du Soleil's strategy.

Marketing Festivals, Consumer Shows, and Fairs

Some of these events fall into the category of impulse or short-term planning. While the promoter or organizer wants to get advance sales of tickets, it is not probable that consumers will plan ahead for some of these events.

Advertising	The sponsor can tag the end of its radio or TV commercials, recommending that people go to the event. The sponsor can put discount coupons or reminders about the events at the bottom of its newspapers ads.
Direct Mail	The sponsor can give the marketer mailing lists of potential attendees.
Public Relations	The event marketer can tap into the sponsor's public relations efforts with the sponsor getting extra media coverage for the event.
Sales	The sponsor can sell tickets to the event at the sponsor's locations.

Figure 7-1

Virtually all events provide a myriad of opportunities for sponsors to gain recognition in exchange for their support. The sponsor must see a return on investment (ROI) as a result of the sponsorship investment made in order to continue support.

Marketing for these events requires not only working with sponsors and media, but also realizing the many resources needed to promote special events. As stated earlier in Chapter 4, sponsors and media can be utilized to help make events even more successful. Figure 7-1 shows how a sponsor might contribute to an event.

Media Sponsors and Events

The media play an important role in marketing events. The media face stiff competition from other media outlets, both print and electronic, and one way to set themselves apart is to become a media sponsor of events in their community. WRC-TV, the NBC affiliate in Washington, DC, realizes the importance of this type of sponsorship. On one three-day weekend in October, the station was the official media sponsor of AIDS Walk, Taste of DC, and the Rock N Race. With the use of on-site signage and banners as well as news personalities on site, the television station demonstrated its commitment to the community while setting itself apart from the competition. How much does this cost the media? Typically, advertisements are placed into time slots that have not been sold or station promotional mentions are aired, which don't count as advertisements, thus not depriving the media of revenue. The media can help play a critical role as unsold advertisement inventory can be used to ensure awareness of events.

PRINT

Instead of white space appearing in a publication's advertisements, sponsorship advertisements can be inserted. Thus, depending on how many advertisements are in a day's paper, the event advertisements can be inserted on a space-available basis.

RADIO

A common promotional vehicle for fairs, festivals, and other special events is working with the promotion department of a radio station to become a partner in an event. Typically, one radio station will want exclusivity as the radio partner or sponsor and, in exchange, will work with the promoter to market the event to the public. The radio station will run a series of commercials, promotional spots, and, in some cases for nonprofit entities, public service announcements. To add more credibility and enhancement, radio personalities from the stations either act as emcees to the events or appear live at the events to give away radio promotional materials or, in some cases, autographs.

For the National Race for the Cure, an adult contemporary station is the exclusive radio sponsor and, as part of its commitment, the station continuously promotes the event as its major radio promotion for the year. The station is credited by the organizers with helping to make the race the largest 5K in the world with over 60,000 runners. If the event is broad enough and big enough, more than one radio station can be brought on for each category of audience. This might include formats such as news/talk, Top 40, urban, adult contemporary, and rock.

TELEVISION

Besides broadcasting advertisements and promotions on television, the TV station can integrate the event into its news coverage, by doing actual news stories about the event and also coordinating "live shots" at the event. For example, at an annual food event attended by over one million people and as part of its partnership, a local television station runs stories about the event in advance. Then live newscasts occur during the events. The station could also have a booth at the event in which it promotes its personalities or programming.

The Perfect Blend: Advertising, Public Relations, and Promotion

The true success to marketing special events, concerts, and festivals is to combine the strengths of advertising, public relations, and promotion to reinforce the special event. To implement a successful marketing campaign, a marketer must create aspects of advertising, public relations, and promotion that complement each other. The key is to time the advertising to create awareness in

Would You Kiss a Boat?

For the Pennsylvania Boat Show, we created a promotion in which a contest was held and 10 listeners of a radio station were invited to come out to the show and kiss a boat continuously. The last person left kissing the boat won it. The promotion took place over a three-day period and was continually advertised by the radio station, as well as in all advertisements placed for the boat show. This helped to create a situation, which was ripe for public relations. Through press releases and the awareness created from the advertising, stories on television, in newspapers, and even on a competing radio station, a wide audience was obtained.

conjunction with a public relations campaign in order to maximize impact. Promotions should be incorporated into the marketing mix. In some cases, a promotion can be publicized by advertising the promotion in order to create awareness.

Street Promotions and Other Unique Promotions

When thinking of a stunt or street promotion, you have to realize that it requires more careful preparation while still making the promotion noteworthy and interesting. Remember, to make the promotion successful, you have to keep it legal. Additionally, location of the promotion is critical; if you are doing the promotion for public attention, pick a central location or an area that has high visibility and large amounts of traffic.

Every year, to announce the fact that the Ringling Bros. and Barnum & Bailey circus is in town, the circus does a street promotion called the animal walk. Depending on logistics and neighborhoods, most of the animals from the circus are paraded from the circus train to the venue in which they will be performing. This is a tradition in every town the circus tours and has been going on for many years. Three years ago, to enhance the excitement,

Ringling Bros. and Barnum & Bailey created an old-fashioned circus parade, similar to the ones that occurred over 50 years ago, featuring circus performers, animals from the show, old circus wagons, marching bands, and lots of horses.

To get attention, you sometimes have to be unique and creative. As people see increasingly outrageous TV shows and contests, marketers have to continue to stand out to grab the attention of their target market.

When planning a street promotion, you must consider weather, risk, and outside influences that might disrupt the stunt. Not everyone may be as excited as you about your promotion. If it is raining, you may not draw as many spectators as you had expected. If the promotion causes traffic jams, the people stuck in traffic will have other thoughts about your promotion.

People love to get something for free, whether it is big or small, so when you think of street promotions all it may take for a little attention is to give something away to the public. By giving away something for free, you guarantee some type of interest and excitement. Make sure the "freebie" has a connection to the event; it

Baby, It's Cold Outside!

You have to be careful about how wild your stunts can be. When you come out of a successful brainstorming session, there may be a temptation to do a stunt or street promotion that may be too bizarre or may not be legal. You have to remember that if something goes wrong or the stunt alienates the public, there may be more negative attention or publicity that could then end up harming the event.

To promote the opening of a boat show, which took place in the middle of the winter, we got one wacky person to water-ski with just a bathing suit on the almost-frozen river that borders the city. In the end, we were lucky our water-skier did not fall into the freezing waters, which could have produced a dangerous situation. He did not, and we saw hundreds pull over to the side of the road, a little confused as they watched him perform tricks in front of photographers and reporters.

Sometimes There Is a Free Lunch!

The agency in charge of the grand-opening events for the Vanity Fair Factory Outlet Malls wanted to create awareness in the media that there was something special inside the shopping center. To accomplish this, the agency ran a promotion: For the four days of the grand opening, the mall would be giving away a free pair of Lee jeans (made by Vanity Fair) to the first 400 people who came through the door. Each day, there was a line of more than 400 people, stretching almost the length of three football fields, all camping out on beach chairs and blankets before the doors even opened. To the media who passed by and saw a huge line every morning, their only impression was that there must be something going on inside the new store. To the traffic reporters who saw traffic jams on the nearby roads, they reported on a "new hot store that has lines before it even opens."

should also have a message on it that promotes the event. Sometimes the act of giving something away can be used to get media coverage.

Whenever there is a chance to win a large sum of money or a trip to an exotic location, people will be attracted in large numbers. Also, if there is a chance for someone to win a car or a million dollars, both the public and the media will take notice. But, remember, by holding one of these contests, you will create a lot of awareness as well as a lot of disappointed people who did not win. As a result, you may damage your event.

In 1990, Foot Locker created the first Million Dollar Shot, which took place during the rookie game at the NBA's All-Star Weekend. One person was chosen at random that year to take a half-court shot for the million dollars. National publicity prior to the event included a story on the front page of *USA Today* and an appearance on the *Late Show with David Letterman*. When the winner, a 15-year-old boy, missed the big shot in front of millions of people on TV, his immediate reaction was to cry in the arms of his parents. The public's reaction to his crying was not the best publicity for Foot Locker.

CELEBRITY AND VIP INVOLVEMENT

The use of celebrities and VIPs at events and festivals can be a beneficial factor in raising the success of a special event. Well-matched celebrities can add credibility and enhance image.

For example, when you have a big-name athlete or Hollywood star, the public associates that with the event and perceives the event as first class in nature. This may help differentiate the event from others, enabling the event organizer to attract more sponsors as well as use the celebrities for hospitality purposes. In addition, celebrities can draw media coverage as the media is always looking for celebrity appearances. The annual Best Buddies Ball, a charity event that raises money for programs for the mentally challenged every year, brings in a star-studded cast to mingle with the attendees. When the media is alerted to the fact that Muhammad Ali, Kevin Spacey, and Helen Hunt are in town, there is extensive national and local interest and coverage by the media.

However, celebrities can cause problems. They do not always listen to instructions, promote the right sponsor, or give the proper message. You, as a marketer, have to do research and talk to others who have used the celebrities in the past. The celebrity's agent is looking for the bookings and may not always tell you the whole story regarding his or her client.

When you have celebrities, you need to maximize their use. By doing advance media with the celebrities before they arrive in town, you can help create the extra excitement that makes for a successful event. When the celebrities are in town, they can do live TV interviews from the venue, stop by TV stations the morning of the event, or do a photo shoot at the venue. By setting up a predinner reception or a luncheon with sponsors or VIPs, you can add to the viability of having the celebrity at the event. The organizer can take instant photos with sponsors and VIPs and then get personal autographs, which can go a long way into making the sponsors sign up again in the years to come.

Although having a celebrity may get everyone excited, the bigger the star, the harder it is to handle and control the influence he or she will have on the event. If it is important for the star to know the details of your event and praise the sponsor, you may look to a star that is less famous but more cooperative. When working with major stars, you have to do intense preparation. Do not assume that the celebrity, equipped with just a brief description of his or her "role," will perform all the duties that are required. Be prepared to give the celebrity a crash course on why he or she is at an event, what he or she will do, background on the program, as well as a briefing of the sponsors and other VIPs involved in the event. This can mean sending background information or a brief video to the celebrity one to two weeks prior to the event. Then a member of the event staff should accompany the car or limousine that is picking up the celebrity. This person should carry 3 × 5 cards with brief points and information on the event. He or she should also have a brief video that can be shown to the celebrity in the car, followed by a summary of the events and a question-and-answer period.

You Get What You Pay For!

The saying goes you get what you pay for and, when using celebrities, this is often the case. Celebrities do not like to say no to public appearances, but they do like to be compensated. Celebrities are also more responsible when they are being paid to be at an event. Many events have had a celebrity donate his or her services, only to cancel at the last minute. A number of years ago, a promoter organized a charity tennis tournament. He looked around town to find an honorary chairman—a high-profile celebrity who played tennis and would lend credibility to the event. The promoter did some research and discovered that a popular local news anchor was an avid tennis player. The promoter contacted the news anchor, who agreed not only to serve as the honorary chairman but, more important, to play in a lunchtime celebrity tennis match against one of the event's sponsors. A week before the event, the promoter confirmed the celebrity's participation, but when it came time for the tennis match, the celebrity did not show up, disappointing all the participants who were looking forward to meeting him and watching him play tennis. However, during the past two years, the promoter has paid over 200 celebrities to make appearances at his events and in only two cases has he had no-shows.

On occasion, using a local VIP such as a politician may be desirable to attract attention and add credibility to an event. You must be careful when using politicians as they may bring in people and add credibility, but they also may bring controversy. In addition, although the program may call for a brief speech, politicians sometimes do not know the meaning of the word "brief." For the Annual Help the Homeless Walkathon, the event was scheduled to start at 10:00 A.M. with brief speeches by sponsors and politicians for 20 minutes. The event organizers were prepared for the walk to start at 10:20 A.M. with hundreds of event staff in place. At 10:40, politicians were still rambling on, and in order to get the event going, organizers had to literally walk on the stage and cut off the last speech.

Branding Your Event

The most famous branded event is the Olympic Games. The branding of this event is so important that, unless a company is a sponsor of the Olympic Games, it cannot use the term "Olympic Games" in any advertising. In fact, the Olympic Games protects its name to such a high degree that the Olympic committees even trademark other similar names, such as the Sydney Committee for the Olympic Games (SOCOG). The goal of an event organizer is to have a branded event that is so popular that the mere mention of the name brings instant recognition, awareness, and attention.

After putting together a successful event, others may look at that event and say, "We could do one better" or, "There is a big market for this type of event. Why don't I get my piece of the pie by duplicating the event?" The important thing to remember is that now, by creating a name, a logo, and a concept, all with trademark protection, you can brand the event. There are many circuses across the country, including Ringling Bros. and Barnum & Bailey—the world's largest, but when the Canadian circus troupe Cirque du Soleil came up with a unique, artistic, nonanimal, avantgarde circus, it became a success. To make sure that Cirque du Soleil kept its market, it quickly set up year-round versions in Las Vegas, Orlando, and Louisiana, in addition to its traveling troupes. Not content to sit back and lose that part of the market, Ringling Bros. created its own one-tent circus, Barnum's Kaleidoscope, in an attempt to compete against Cirque du Soleil.

To secure the branded event, a marketer must create an identity both graphically and descriptively. The first phase is creating a logo. Today, corporations can spend upwards of a million dollars to create a logo. They do this because a logo creates an image that one respects and understands, and this helps brand the event. The public may stay away from something unfamiliar. Just look at the success of McDonald's and T.G.I. Friday's. Although they are popular in all their locations with respect to product, they deliver consistency in a package that large numbers of people want. The same can be said about events and festivals. If there is a successful branded event in one area or during a specific time of year, the public will come to trust in the event, guaranteeing the longevity of the enterprise.

Guerrilla Marketing of Festivals and Special Events

Guerrilla marketing involves the use of unorthodox and sometimes unusual methods whereby marketers try to get attention for their events in front of a built-in audience. Since there are so many efforts to reach the target markets of events by using traditional media, you have to look for unique ideas to draw attention to the festival or event. Consumers are assaulted by hundreds of advertising messages per day. Through the use of guerrilla marketing, you can make your advertising message and event identifiable. This can also be called "in-your-face" marketing because one takes immediate notice of the guerrilla-marketing tactics. In order for guerrilla tactics to succeed, you must have the element of surprise, create attention by doing something unique, have something that is attention getting to promote, and find an area where there already is a large built-in audience. When you have these elements, you can successfully pull off a guerrilla-marketing exercise.

An increasing number of mainstream marketers are using guerrilla-marketing tactics to draw attention. It is not unusual to see free samples of new soft drinks or candy bars being given away in congested areas of major downtown cities, but as more marketers do this, this type of marketing will lose some of its edge.

Measurement Methods

Determining whether a festival, fair, or other special event has been successful can take many different approaches. First, a marketer needs to identify the goals. If you are looking to raise awareness for a cause, the organizer will typically interview attendees prior to and during the event as well as at the conclusion. Typically, at these events, organizations are looking for volunteers at the event, while at the same time disseminating information about the cause. By interviewing individuals who are familiar with the event and the cause, we can gain an insight into the approximate number of people interviewed, informed, and successfully solicited for volunteer positions. From this comes not only a parameter of participation statistics, but also general feedback regarding attitudes and interest levels.

When one is trying to promote goodwill in a community such as having a Fourth of July fireworks festival or an open house at the local fire station, one looks to feedback from the community in local newspapers or on talk radio shows, as well as doing random interviews with people in the community. In some cases, one can judge by increasing attendance as the festivals become larger. At fundraising events, the bottom line is how much money was raised for the cause, as well as how many people were recruited to raise more funds on their own. When looking to see how successfully a sponsor's name has been promoted, one can look at the advertising and public relations and assign these two a value. For advertising, wherever a sponsor's name or logo is used prominently, an advertising value can be determined by obtaining advertisement rates for the specific advertisements run and then combining the costs of all the advertisements. On the public relations side, one can look at the comparative advertising value. This figure is obtained by collecting all press clips of the event where a sponsor is mentioned or featured in photos and determining what this would cost if one had to pay for all of the exposure.

Summary

Festivals, fairs, and other special events differ from association and corporate events in nature. To successfully market your event, you must carefully designate and take advantage of the unique qualities of the event. Traditional media, such as television, radio, and print, can contribute to the event marketing to a great extent, especially when you find any correlation with the niche media. Marketing these special events requires not only traditional methods, but also nontraditional marketing techniques, such as street promotion and guerrilla marketing. These unconventional methods are apt to attract attention from the public and often result in media exposure. The perception of the public and the coverage by the media, however, are not always positive. Thus, a marketer should understand that unusual approaches are always accompanied by risks as well as opportunities. Using appropriate celebrities and VIPs in your event gives your event certain credibility and prestige, in addition to the media exposure and enhanced sponsor relationships. On the other hand, it is essential for the marketer to educate the celebrities and VIPs and communicate their tasks to them. Ultimately, how special your event can be is dependent on branding. Festivals, fairs, and other special events, as well as other tangible products, need a strong branding. A powerful branding can clearly distinguish your event from millions of other, similar events. Overall, marketing is an endless effort. Today's success does not guarantee tomorrow's. Therefore, it is important for a marketer to set a goal, review and evaluate its success, and change the marketing strategy accordingly.

TALES FROM THE FRONT

In 2000, NBC's *Today Show* co-host Katie Couric decided to get together with Lilly Tartikoff, widow of former NBC head Brandon Tartikoff, to create a brand-new special event to raise awareness and funds for colon cancer research. Ms. Couric's husband, Jay Monahan, died in 1998 from the affliction and she was looking to do something to make a difference in battling the disease. Ms. Couric and Ms. Tartikoff looked around at all of the big charity events in the United States and saw that there were already many charity runs and walks across the country. They realized that they wanted to create a big event, but it had to be different. They both had relationships with celebrities and musicians that might add something extra to a fundraising walk or run. They developed the idea of having a 5K walk featuring some celebrity friends of theirs as well as ending the event with a postwalk concert. They then tied in with the Entertainment Industry Foundation and created one of the nation's most successful first-time events.

After research, it was discovered that colon cancer typically attacks men and women aged 40 years and older. The target was to reach this audience. The event was to take place in Washington, DC, because it was the hometown of Katie Couric and also because political efforts could be pushed to coincide with the event.

Event organizers coordinated advertising promotional support from the *Washington Post* and WRQX-FM, an adult contemporary radio station. The paper agreed to give them free space-available ads to support the event. The first ads appeared two months prior to the event with a push on getting people to register to walk and to solicit pledges. Then two weeks prior to the event, the ads in the paper started to reflect the entertainment side of the event. The *Washington Post* contributed over $100,000 in advertising support. The radio station ran ads and public service announcements for a two-month period, totaling over $30,000 in value.

Four major sponsors were brought on board, each receiving signage at the event,

logo placement in print ads, and VIP hospitality at the event as well as announcements during the event. Sponsors were also interviewed and reported on by the media. While ads were reaching the papers and radio, Katie Couric, TV star Dennis Franz, and baseball star Eric Davis were doing interviews with the *Washington Post* and numerous radio stations. To elicit excitement about the event, there were registration parties at Bloomingdales, one of the event sponsors. Because of Ms. Couric's connections, Dennis Franz from *NYPD Blue;* Eric Davis from the St. Louis Cardinals, who had recovered from colon cancer; and the singer Paul Simon were brought on board. This helped to make this event a high-profile occasion, as well as a major musical extravaganza. Because of the success of the first year—over 25,000 walkers and over 100,000 concertgoers—preparations are now going forward to continue this event in Washington, DC, and possibly in other cities.

Chapter Challenge

1. Describe how you would use the media and the value-added promotions tied in with the media to promote a new Hispanic circus in the community.

2. List three promotions that you would use to promote a corporate golf tournament/classical music concert.

CHAPTER 8

Trends in Event Marketing

How can we know the future? Conjure it like Merlin, study it like an astronomer, or divine it like a fortune teller? Perhaps we can only deduce it, like Sherlock Holmes?

—THE FUTURIST, JULY–AUGUST 2001

WHEN YOU HAVE COMPLETED THIS CHAPTER, YOU WILL BE ABLE TO:

- Identify the leading trends that will affect your future event marketing efforts
- Understand and use future event marketing methods in convention, corporate, exposition, festival, social, and other events
- Determine the best future practices in reaching your target market in the most efficient and high-impact manner
- Develop scenarios for future event marketing programs relevant to changing demographics and psychographics
- Improve your event marketing segmentation skills
- Refine your event marketing evaluation methods
- Develop and implement new, cutting-edge event marketing strategies to beat your competition

The modern event marketer must constantly develop and use his or her detective skills, much like the legendary Sherlock Holmes, to reveal the mysteries that event marketing may hold in the next several decades. While it is impossible to be 100 percent accurate regarding the future of event marketing, it is also essential that professional event marketers study fads, trends, statistics, and other critical information to anticipate the changes that will ultimately affect their ability to efficiently and effectively market events in the future.

Leading Trends in Event Marketing

Edward Cornish, editor of the *Futurist* magazine, believes that "on a day-to-day basis, the world changes so slowly that the best way to predict tomorrow is to say that it will be like today." However, although today's events may be used as a barometer to historically track developments and forecast trends, the professional event marketer must also keep his or her eye focused on the future needs, wants, and desires of event guests. By anticipating future needs, the event marketer can influence demand and fill those needs with events that are essential to human productivity and well-being. Figure 8-1 lists the ten leading trends in event marketing that will result from future lifestyle, demographic, and cultural changes.

The tragic events of September 11, 2001, forever changed the psyche of those who travel and gather for events. The resulting cancellations of events and downturn in attendance for those that were held in the weeks after the terrorist attacks compelled new strategies for event marketing. Event marketers must now be involved with issues of security, emergency planning, and rapid response to negative public reaction in times of national crisis. Critical to this is the need to put these issues in perspective for potential audiences and to reassure attendees that their security needs are being met. Safety and security have become part of the marketing message. Emphasis must be placed on the continuing need to gather, and to benefit from the experience of the event and the relationships developed with those who attend.

These trends represent hundreds of micro developments occurring on a global scale in the economy, in technology, and in lifestyles, including health and wellness. The experienced professional event marketer will continually monitor these trends and determine how to adapt his or her marketing plan and product/service to fill these future needs.

Ten Event Marketing Influencers and Resulting Trends

Influencer	Trend
Aging demographics	Larger print will be used for brochures and other text.
More disposable income	The number of events before and immediately after the main event will be increased to capture more revenue while the guest is at the destination.
Improved technological delivery	Video streaming on the World Wide Web will be used to demonstrate speakers, entertainment, recreation, and other benefits of attending the event.
Faster technology	Real-time registration will be available 24 hours a day, 7 days a week with instant confirmation and special financial benefits for early registration through yield management software.
New media outlets	Advertising will extend to nontraditional sites such as schools, clubs, offices, rest rooms, amusement parks, and other venues where guests may experience a wait time.
New vocabulary	Copy writers will begin to use the slang and jargon practiced by visitors to chat rooms on the World Wide Web and will avoid "scammers" and "flamers" and embrace key buzz words popular within the netster generation.
Emphasis on health benefits	As the population ages, the need for work/ vacations will increase. Therefore, event marketers will stress the health, recreation, and well-being aspects of the event.
Seamless registration	Transportation, accommodation, registration, and ancillary tours will be available through central Web sites to capture as much revenue as possible from each individual guest.
Multilingual communication	Instant translation software will provide prospective event guests with a choice of languages to respond to the event offer and make registration and ticket sales a global enterprise with no barriers to non-English speakers.
Terrorism alerts	Focus messages on safety and security where appropriate and emphasize the need to be there to benefit fully from the event.

Figure 8-1 A careful analysis of attendee needs and lifestyles, as well as the level of financial and sociopolitical resources represented, will directly influence the creation of precise marketing strategies.

Individual Event Marketing Methods

Event Type	Marketing Method	Result (Return on Event Marketing Measurement)
Convention	World Wide Web	Improved early registration and increased sales of other event products (such as tours, special events) through targeted marketing due to data base analysis.
Festival	Nontraditional media	Use of doctors' offices, hospitals, and pharmacies to market health and wellness festivals, use of sport venues to market classical and other highbrow musical events will produce higher yield in ticket sales due to market segmentation and avoidance of clutter from other media as is typical with television, radio, and print advertising.
Exposition	Cooperative advertising	Exhibitors will increasingly become co-marketers as well as event vendors to reduce cost, increase ability to target, and improve yield in attendance.
Education	Affinity marketing	Alumni, friends of the university or school, and other stakeholders will become ambassadors or influencers to refer qualified prospective students or event attendees in order to provide strong third-party endorsement and reduce risk of attendee disappointment.
Social	World Wide Web and Telephony	The World Wide Web will be used to promote attendance at a wide range of social events, the Web will be integrated with the telephone system to provide real-time chat capability at reduced cost, and the integration of the Web and television will allow event guests to preview, select, and then review activities taking place before, during, and after the event.

Figure 8-2
The nature of the event itself may dictate the marketing methods selected. The event marketer will set a strategy of identifying avenues of communication and influence to attract attention and registrations.

Future Event Marketing Methods

As a direct result of the influencers shown in Figure 8-1, event marketers must begin to employ new techniques to reach event attendees in a cost-effective, high-impact way. To generate the greatest return on event marketing (ROEM), event marketers and their stakeholders must use different methods to reach individual event markets as shown in Figure 8-2.

Therefore, whether you are marketing a social event or the Olympic Games, your paradigm is about to change. This change will occur as you carefully research your target market and then carefully and thoughtfully, as well as skillfully, develop and implement your marketing strategy. While it is possible to borrow marketing methods from one type of event and use them within the context of another, each type of event generally requires a precise marketing strategy that enables you to rapidly capture the attention of your target market, quickly and thoroughly provide them with enough information to make a positive decision, and then effortlessly influence them to invest in your event. It is essential that you become an expert in the type of event that you are about to market just as an auto mechanic specializes in specific vehicles and a doctor specializes in specific maladies. As a professional event marketer in the 21st century, you must not only be a generalist, but also a knowledgeable specialist in your event field.

How to Determine the Best Future Practices in Reaching Your Target Market

As you contemplate your future marketing plans, you must ask three important questions: (1) How can I reduce the length of time from event development to market success? (2) How can I cut through the marketing clutter to differentiate my event product? (3) How can I reduce the cost of making each sale? The reason you must ask these questions is because your employer, stakeholders, supervisors, and others are asking these questions before you even consider writing the event marketing plan. They want to know how you will market this event faster, better, and more profitably. Whether you are a for-profit or a not-for-profit organization, the demands remain the same. To be competitive, you must pose and

	Faster, Better, More Profitable
Challenge	**Potential Solution**
Faster	Use the World Wide Web to conduct continuous virtual focus groups to build demand and target your message.
Better	Utilize nontraditional marketing partners to improve your marketing message delivery and reach new segments.
More Profitable	Utilize sponsors to reduce marketing cost; implement vital marketing through the Web to generate word-of-mouth interest through targeted chat rooms and newsgroups.

Figure 8-3

Marketing is a major, if not *the* major, expense item for many events. It is incumbent upon the marketer to determine the most cost- and time-effective methods of reaching the target audiences.

clearly answer these questions. Figure 8-3 provides some examples of how to do this faster, better, and with greater profit.

Successful event marketers in the 21st century understand how to quickly, effectively, and profitably respond to or create demand for their event. It is essential that you continually keep your ear and eye close to your target and emerging target markets to learn how to quickly influence them to attend your event. If you are late, or provide poor quality, or do not achieve a satisfactory profit margin, your event competitors are waiting in the wings to capture the market you have left behind.

How to Develop Scenarios for Future Event Marketing Programs

Event risk managers often use scenario planning to forecast potential hazards or hazardous situations. Event marketers must also use scenarios to determine how to anticipate and, therefore, be prepared for challenges and opportunities that may disrupt or enhance their event marketing plan. Figure 8-4 provides five sample

Scenarios and Action Steps

Scenarios	Action Steps
Economic downturn occurs in community six months before festival opens.	Work with the office of economic development to provide services at the festival to stimulate employment, foster business-to-business development, and promote the economic impact of the festival. Offer family passes at reduced rates to decrease single-ticket cost and raise overall per capita spending from food, drink, and souvenir purchases.
Major military action is announced before event.	Offer discounts for military personnel, veterans, and their families to promote patriotic spirit of your organization.
Major competitor announces that it will hold its exposition one week after yours is held.	Differentiate your event from the other through testimonials from previous attendees and endorsements from leading experts. Offer deep discounts for early registration.
Energy costs rise and reduce auto travel for those who would otherwise attend your event.	Promote in conjunction with transportation companies alternative transit to your event, including bus tours, rail travel, and air packages. Demonstrate savings to ticket buyers in all advertising. Offer discounts to guests who use public and other alternative forms of transportation.
Negative media stories circulate about your event's safety record and economic losses.	Anticipate and promote positive statistics about your event through spokespersons, testimonials, industry experts, and others. Develop a speaker's bureau to reach out to new groups and spread the good news about your event.

Figure 8-4
At any time, the marketing strategy may be changed by outside influences that impact negatively on the potential attendance. Anticipating such problems and devising response plans will provide for fast, effective action steps.

scenarios and examples of how you can use these scenarios to increase sales for your event.

Obviously, you cannot anticipate every potential problem; however, you can generally outline the most likely conditions that will positively or negatively impact your ability to market your event product. Therefore, it is essential that you have at all times a plan ready to seize potential opportunities and mitigate threats, ensuring that your marketing plan remains stable and successful despite changes brought about by new and emerging scenarios. In the past, event marketers may have said, "I had no control over the company going on strike or three weeks of rain," but, in the 21st century, event marketers must constantly devise these scenarios and be ready to embrace them with strategies to produce successful outcomes.

How to Improve Your Event Marketing Segmentation Skills

The term "market segmentation" can be defined simply as the process of identifying target market groups that may be available for the event marketers' products and services. These segments may already be included within the current targets of the marketing plan in effect, but many may not be. Those that are not often provide the fertile fields of growth and revitalization of the event itself.

Throughout this text, you have been alerted to the self-defeating tendency of repetition, whether it involves program design, promotional tools, speakers, event features, or marketing lists. The clear trend in event marketing is toward a shining of the light into new areas filled with innovative design opportunities and, even more important, consumers who are currently not being recruited. Those consumers may be off of your "radar screen," but they also may be operating much closer to you than you think.

Markets continually change, as do their tastes, interests, fads, and priorities. For example, many companies have faced flagging sales because they did not see the trends in their markets evolving. In every economic downturn, observers will see the sad cycle of those corporations that became too comfortable in the sanctity of their profitability and failed to stay ahead of the consumer curve and the incessant changes in desire and demand of their markets. When that happens, inventories rise as customer demand shifts to new and more attractive product offerings by competitors, discounts are offered to move products, and per unit profits fall. The message that the corporate event marketer conveys must reflect the challenges of overcoming this regression—and righting the ship—and the strategic plans of management for accomplishing this.

This is no less true for the association event marketer. Association memberships should reflect the industries and professions that they represent. Be alerted that there is no guarantee that they do, without an effective marketing plan to continually analyze changes in market segments and the direct influence they have on event participation. A striking example of this is the growth of megastores in the retail industry, dramatically (and often woefully) changing the landscape of the memberships that support the associations representing them. In the hardware industry, thousands of small family-owned stores have disappeared as huge retail outlets have opened either in malls or as stand-alone retailers throughout the United States. The same can be seen in the drug retail industry, the printing industry, the office supply industry, among many others.

Bear in mind that, as years go by, certain types of consumers and their values fade as new ones emerge. These "psychographic" profiles, used to identify buyer values and priorities, will often influence the decision whether or not to buy, attend, and participate.

For example, the World War II and Baby Boomer generations have been identified by their value of long-lasting relationships, institutional and personal loyalty, permanent relationships, and patience. A chat over the nuts and bolts in the hardware store may not have been efficient or time effective, but was long a valued and venerable phenomenon of the community psyche throughout the nation and its towns.

Now emerging in the marketplace are the maturing Generation Xers and evolving Generation Next markets. They present characteristics that are markedly different. Raised in the instant-response environment of faxes, e-mails, and online messaging, they expect instant results. They, in large measure, don't want to "wait in line." They scoff at "snail mail." In general, they are multitaskers eager to accomplish several objectives at once, not given to good people skills, and in relationships with casual acquaintances. And they tend to be highly impatient and somewhat skeptical. They exhibit a desire to make each minute count at work and play. The marketer must be aware that they do not trust a newspaper article or promotional piece simply because they see something in print "so it must be true." The challenge to convince this market is great.

Thus, the one-stop shopping syndrome permeates our marketplaces to a growing degree. Whether it is shopping at a megastore or attending an educational or social event, the time must be well spent and beneficial. "What will I learn?" "Who will I meet?" "How will I benefit?" For the marketer, these are *key issues* to address in promotion. And the *keyword* is "I."

Event marketers have the same issues with which to deal. Are attendance trends at the annual Veteran's Day parade up, down, or stagnant? Are sponsorships in demand or declining? Which community precincts are conspicuous by their representation? Which are not? The marketing executive responsible for the annual community awards and recognition gala must be equally investigative. Is attendance growing? Are essentially the same people coming each year? If so, are they growing older, retiring, becoming less influential than in years before? Are our newer markets being overlooked, both as attendees and as honorees?

Many marketers have found, too late and to their dismay, that by catering to old standbys and ignoring emerging markets they were "ringing the tree" (an old saying that, when you cut a small ring around the base of a tree's bark, nutrients will be blocked from the roots and in time the tree will wither and die). Many events have faded away because new markets were not segmented, identified, and embraced to supply continuing nutrition and support.

As a marketer, you should not pursue new markets until you have identified and analyzed the markets you currently attract and the trends that create the ebb and flow of the buyers and attendees you seek. Using the qualitative and quantitative research techniques already described in this text, market segmentation begins with identifying, qualifying, and prioritizing the consumers you serve. In others words, "who is coming to your party?"

In addition to the standard demographics such as age, gender, annual income, years of event attendance, and many others described in Chapter 2, more definitive and probing questions are being used as marketers improve their segmentation skills. Figure 8-5 represents questions used in a research instrument searching for greater audience definition. The instrument can be both qualitative and quantitative in design.

Samples of Qualitative and Quantitative Survey Questions

Attendee Information
- Name, Address, Contact Numbers (Optional)
- What is your profession?
- What is your professional title?
- How long have you been in the business?
- Which of the past 10 years have you attended? (Provide check-off list)
- Why have you attended in those years? Rate on a scale of 1–10 all that apply. Add any other reasons important to you.
  1. Social Events
  2. Education/Professional Development
  3. Peer Networking/Interaction
  4. Travel
  5. Combine with Vacation
  6. See New Products at the Exposition
  7. Find New Markets for My Product
  8. Pursue My Leadership Role in Organization
  9. Pre- and Postevent Tours
  10. Attraction of the Event Venue/Location
  11. Celebrity Attractions/Entertainment
  12. Test the Pulse of the Industry, Study Trends
  13. Gather Information About New Competitors
  14. Find a Better Job/Become Upwardly Mobile
  15. Review New Professional Literature/Research

Figure 8-5
This example of a survey instrument includes both quantitative and qualitative items. Key to this approach is to make the questionnaire long enough to gain the information most important to the marketing effort, and short enough that the target will take the time to respond.

The list is limited only by the marketer's need to know and his or her imaginative creativity. Obviously, the length of the questionnaire will impact the time the respondent is willing to spend on the exercise. Therefore, *need to know* is a critical ingredient. As a marketer, you must first define what informational goals are most important to the research and construct the instrument with those goals in mind.

Many such surveys are tabulated, recorded, reviewed with passive interest, and then ignored. The scrupulous investigator, however, matches the queries and responses through "comparative analysis" to gain insight into emerging markets. For example, the question "How long have you been in the business?" is key to identifying an emerging group of buyers. Responses of one, two, or three years should be compared with subentry 14 to determine a relationship between this demographic group and the desire to improve one's job status. If the match is positive and significant, the marketing message to promote to this potential constituency is clear.

On the other hand, let us assume that the vast majority of the respondents represent long-time attendees and veterans and alarmingly few are newcomers to the playing field. This may well mean that the event has reached an age nexus that portends an eventual "passing of the guard," with no new markets being attracted to replenish the event and the organization itself.

This is a classic marketing challenge. It is *not* a nightmare for the marketer. Rather, it is a great *opportunity*. As the marketer, you will want to work with program planners to design events that will attract new participants, and then craft promotional messages and methods that will enlist the participation of a whole new market. And, as the marketer, you may have saved not only the long-term future of the organization's events, but also perhaps the future of the organization as a viable entity.

Figure 8-6 presents still more questions the marketing executive needs to answer in studying trends in new market segments. They probe more behavioral profiles and values. These issues typically require qualitative approaches and may be applied to smaller groups that can be urged to assure adequate response (such as corporate managers, franchise owners, or association elected leaders). Still, questions still may be asked of the more casual constituent, depending on need. The queries illustrated in Figure 8-6 are more

---

Personal/Business Profile Questions

- How many purchases did you make last year (in dollar volume) as a result of contacts made at our exhibit?
- When do you make your buying plans?
- What do you buy? What may you buy in the future?
- What dollar volume of purchases are you personally responsible for in a fiscal year?
- What do you see as the greatest challenge to your success?
- What do you see as your greatest educational need?
- If you had your choice, where would you most like assistance? (Time management, office systems, administrative assistance, distributor communications, identifying customer needs.)
- What industry publications do you read regularly?
- What other publications do you read regularly?
- What television programs do you watch regularly?
- Would you be willing to serve as a "network marketer" for our event in your community? (If so, indicate name and contact information.)

Figure 8-6
A qualitative survey instrument may be used for general information about target markets not necessarily related to a specific event. In many cases, new events can be designed as a result of better understanding of new market segments.

intimate and in depth than the previous, but may reveal significant insights into new marketing approaches.

Why ask questions such as these? Who needs to know? Exhibitors will want to know the buying power of your audience. Advertisers will want to know who makes buying decisions, and what publications your attendees read, in order to strategize advertising design and placement. Key speakers and sponsors will want to know the experience level of their audiences and the positions they hold in their companies. As the marketer, you need to know your markets as intimately as possible in order to persuade your program participants, as well as attendees, to gather.

Always bear in mind that a market segment need not be a question of sheer numbers to be vital. Even more important in certain instances is the *influence* that this market segment brings to the table. As we have said earlier, asking personal questions and soliciting opinions of the "movers and shakers" in an industry or association instills a sense of proprietary interest among them. When those leaders feel that interest in the mission, the task of the marketer in approaching their followers will be greatly facilitated.

Refining Your Event Marketing Evaluation Methods

The trends in effective marketing evaluation point directly at efficient record keeping (archiving), documentation, and evaluation of virtually every element of the event. Overall attendance is good to know and easy to track. Attendance at *each* event function is *better* to know and more difficult to track. The answers lead to clear indications of attendee preferences and needs and will result in modifications (sometimes subtle, sometimes dramatic) in the marketing message and event programming. How are performance records documented?

DOCUMENTATION

In establishing a system of event performance archives, remember this basic principle: Keep records of virtually everything, from the beginning of the marketing process through the event's final evaluations. Sophisticated computer programs may help you retain and recoup the records in an organized fashion—in perpetuity—for examination and comparison at critical junctures of the planning process. But computers can only provide the information that is gathered for input, and only to the degree of accuracy with which the data are measured.

The marketer should keep copies of absolutely everything connected with the campaign, together with mailing or transmission dates as well as response levels for each medium. Dates of the responses are also important. Translating the history of the event is critical. For event planners, it is vital to know if the sponsoring organization enjoys immediate and positive responses to promotion. Planning is much easier when the early acceptance of the invitation (and the number of registrations) is known early on. But an organization whose target audience is historically late in registering for an event will be presented with other planning and marketing challenges. For example, planning is possible (if not more stressful) when the respondents typically register during the last few weeks prior to the opening of the event.

There will be dramatic effects on purchasing decisions. For example, negotiating accurate hotel room block cutoffs, obtaining food and beverage guarantees, ordering supplies, and working out logistical details are virtually impossible without a concrete and demonstrable prior history of performance and patterns exhibited by your attendees. That information can come only through collection, archiving, and clear interpretation of those patterns to the satisfaction of the event's suppliers and performers.

Consider these methods of documenting patterns of participation:

1. **Ticket Collection.** Many groups use tickets for admission to major events. Tickets may be collected at doors or at tables. They should be color coded by event (for easier categorizing later), counted, and *kept*. A great failing of many marketers is to collect tickets, bind them together, place them on a shelf in the office for use later in the next marketing campaign, and then forget they are there as they gather dust. They are the old-fashioned, but tried-and-true "hard copy" of attendance profiles.

2. **Hand Counters.** Head counts may be taken by attendants at the entrances to events with the use of hand counters or "clickers." While not as accurate as a ticket collection, they are often used when ticket collection will create delays in event access or meal service.

3. **Observation.** Especially for smaller sessions and break-outs, simple observation of the room during a program will allow a close estimation of the level of attendance, as well as the level of interest by the audience in specific event features or subject areas.

4. **Patterns of Arrival.** For purposes of airline or transit arrivals and adequate preparation of the host facility for manning reservation and registration desks, patterns of arrival must be tracked. This will be impacted by the geographic spread of attendees and the venue location (West Coast/East Coast, for example), days of week, time of day, even down

to hours. For corporate meetings, this is rather routine information because travel arrangements are usually preordained by the company. For fairs, festivals, awards dinners, and association events, the issues become more problematical. Remember that the attendees are not under the control of the sponsoring organization and will make their own travel arrangements. Hotels typically maintain computer records on all aspects of a guest's stay, including arrival times, types of rooms requested, no-shows, on-site purchases, and departure times (including early departures). The event organizer can request a flowchart from the facility's computer with all this information, even on a daily basis, for analysis on site.

5. **Patterns of Departure.** Reversing the data needed for arrival patterns, departure patterns are equally important. If half of the audience is historically gone from the facility before the closing-night banquet, the marketing executive faces a challenge. The solutions may be many: Beefing up the closing-night event, adding postconvention tours and features, or holding a major prize drawing or silent auction are examples of effective responses to the problem. This is a challenge for proactive marketers who can influence program planners for the event.

Regardless of the data to be accumulated and the methods used, these patterns of performance must be archived, maintained, and used to predict future patterns, as well as to improve the marketing strategies and effect more acceptable negotiations with event suppliers.

Data should be organized into charts immediately, in order to analyze results quickly and continually. For example, registrations received should be logged weekly (if not daily) and retained for a "critical path" analysis over a period of years. This will influence promotional timetables and techniques. Attendance at workshops should be charted by topic, time of day, and day of week to establish patterns. Certain topics may not be popular with the audience attracted. On the other hand, they may be popular with audiences *not* being attracted, which raises even more compelling marketing possibilities. Events at resorts often draw participants in healthy numbers in the morning, while attendance falls off in the afternoon due to the lure of golf and tennis. No details are too minute to ignore in gathering and evaluating data on patterns of participation.

DOCUMENTING SUPPORTER IMPACT

The lifeblood of many events is provided by sponsors, exhibitors, speakers, celebrities, industry leaders, and other organizational partners. Providing adequate recognition to them is an integral part of the marketing process, in order to allow them to adequately assess their value of participation. Some of the strategies used may be found in Figure 8-7.

- Have a photographer on hand at their appearances, capturing the dynamics of the occasion as a keepsake to present in a portfolio following the event.
- Have a photographer take photographs of each exhibit booth, either posed or action scenes with exhibit personnel and their buyers in conversation.
- Arrange for interviews of supporters, sponsors, and exhibitors by members of the trade and consumer press, wherever possible. Provision of a press room or speakers' lounge will facilitate this.
- Make copies of all items, news articles, and conference newsletter coverage and advertisements that mention the sponsor and exhibitor. Include these documents in the portfolio.
- Present a plaque, video, certificate of appreciation, or at least a letter of thanks from an organization or corporate leader for the supporter's participation.
- Provide a demographic profile of the audience you provided to the supporter or sponsor, including levels of authority in the company or industry, buying power of the attendees, and laudatory comments from attendees.
- Remind sponsors of the availability of increasing levels of sponsorship and recognition. Encourage them to expand sponsorships in upcoming events.

Figure 8-7
Event supporters look not only for return on investment, but also for *recognition* in front of your audience. Event marketers can do much to ensure that the supporters will be proud of their involvement and ready to come back again.

The Hospitality Sales and Marketing Association International thanks exhibitors and sponsors with a surprise gift during the initial phases of tear-down of the exposition, as well as a personal visit to each booth and thank you by key leaders and staff members. The gifts are normally creative specialty advertising items, bearing a thank-you inscription and a reminder of the dates and location of the next show. Wine and soft drinks are served to make the chore of dismantling the exhibits more palatable. The response of the exhibitors each year is one of appreciation (and amazement in many cases). Such treatment is extremely rare for them, and the goodwill is reflected in a sold-out show three times each year.

Here are five final tips on evaluation methods:

1. Keep copies of all print, video, audio, and other media purchases.
2. Track the effectiveness of each media outlet through coded or coupon response forms. Maintain copies of all print advertising, promotions, press kits, and publicity releases chronologically and enter information about responses noted for each.
3. Verify placement schedules and audited circulation of all print media, including the trade press.
4. Analyze the effectiveness of specialty advertising items and giveaways.
5. Maintain copies and records of all cross-promotions with partners and supporters, as well as references to your event carried in their editorial coverage.

Developing New Marketing Strategies to Beat the Competition

Many casual observers feel that there is no real threat of outside competition for corporate meetings (people are told to go, and they go!), association conventions (after all, it's their only annual convention), county fairs, awards banquets, and community parades. This may be true in some cases, but in many instances it is not.

Corporate meetings compete for loyalty among dealers and distributors who may also carry the products of direct competitors. Association events compete against related associations for the loyalty, time, and investment of their members. A county or city fair may compete against summertime family vacations that draw many potential attendees away from the community or region.

The key to competing for any event is to analyze the competition, which may be direct or subtle, and to respond with marketing strategies to overcome the competition. Obviously, the approaches will vary greatly, depending on the challenges presented by the competition. The following generic examples of analyzing your competition will be helpful.

1. Rate the competition's event in comparison to yours in terms of:

- Cost/price
- Timing
- Program features
- Quantifiable benefits
- Influential players/demographics of audience
- Demand (perceived or real)
- Quality
- Marketing strategies employed
- Attendance trends
- Geographic distribution of venues

These and any other pertinent comparisons should be charted on a grid, comparing your event and that of the competition. The rating system used on each comparison can be any that makes sense to you and your analysts (e.g., a scale of 1 to 10, rating poor to excellent; or a ranking system of "E," "G," "F," and "P" for excellent, good, fair, and poor). The grid will enlighten you as to relative strengths and weaknesses and areas to improve the marketing strategies. Don't overcomplicate the process! List only those elements that are important to you. Use a weighting system that others can understand. Most important, once the analysis is in place, "work the plan!" The more user friendly it is, the greater the chance that it will become a living document during the marketing effort, easy to respond to and relevant to changing market conditions. Maintaining the tool on a computer is most conducive to retrieval and modification, but not essential to the effort. Hand charts will suffice for those who, for whatever reason, find the computer a barrier to easy access and manipulation of comparisons. Then archive the charts for year-to-year reference.

2. Question your own product and markets through your market research and analysis:

- What aspects of direct mail, advertising, and public relations have been most successful? Least successful?
- What event elements are most important for your attendees?
- What event elements attract only light response? Why?
- What target markets generate the least business? Why?
- What new features, unique to the competition, can be added to rejuvenate interest in your areas of weak participation? What old features can be eliminated?
- What additional promotional tools can be used to gain a breakthrough at your next event?

Again, the questions you ask of yourself and your marketing team are open ended and infinite. But ask only those that are meaningful. Resist the urge to overcomplicate and thus confuse and forestall your analysts.

3. Apply the SWOT analysis to all comparisons of competition. Comparing "strengths, weaknesses, opportunities, and threats" will add flesh to the skeleton of your grids and charts and make more meaningful your responses to the otherwise mechanical profiles they display. Marketers often find that pursuing certain audiences is an unprofitable exercise, perhaps maintained only by habit or tradition. "Don't throw good product after bad prospects" is an old, but valuable adage in the marketing field. Before giving up on a market, however, ask another vital question: "How long will these negative market conditions last?" Remember that every organization and industry has life cycles, many with continuous ebbs and flows of *strengths and weaknesses*. These fluid conditions will drive the *opportunities and threats* your marketing efforts will encounter in the long term. "SWOT." Write it down again.

The day of the snake-oil salesman is over. There are no more medicines being sold to crowds over the backs of wagons by transients with no lasting ties to the buying community. Marketing has become as much a science as it has an art. It blends human understanding with scientific analysis and high-tech implementation. It requires marketing practitioners who understand the nuances of these characteristics and are able to integrate them into an effective game plan that identifies, reaches, and *satisfies* consumer and audience values, desires, and needs. In the final analysis, the term "satisfies" is the critical component of any marketing effort. Without customer satisfaction, that is, the delivery of the product as promised, future marketing efforts may prove daunting if not fruitless. It is for this reason that marketing must be considered not as an adjunct but as an integral part of product and event design and the strategic management of the organization itself. Enlightened organizations do this. Those that do not will find in their competitive analyses many more weaknesses than strengths and many more threats than opportunities.

You Are the Future of Event Marketing

According to Barbara Moses, in order to recession-proof your career, you must employ 12 strategies for bad times and good. Moses suggests that individuals must take charge of their careers, ensure their employability, create a fallback position, know their key skills, prepare for areas of competence, market effectively, act type A but be type B, build emotional resilience, stay culturally current, be a compelling communicator, fortify their finances, act like an insider and think like an outsider, and, finally, reward themselves.

These same principles can easily be applied to marketing your organization's event services and products. The event is a living, breathing, albeit temporary business that requires a multifaceted approach to ensure a successful marketing outcome. Moses adds that "whether we have conventional full-time jobs or are contingent, contract, or freelance workers, we are all living and working in the TempWorld. In TempWorld everything shifts."

As a professional event marketer, you are living in a temporary world every moment. The events of 9-11 remind us of how fragile the temporary world has become. Therefore, your ability to use the principles in this book to effectively research, design, plan, coordinate, and evaluate your event marketing strategies will ultimately not only determine your success, but will, in fact, affect the success of many other events as well. You are not only marketing a single event or several events, but are ultimately responsible for helping market the entire event industry. By applying the principles in this book, you are well positioned for the success you deserve. Who knows, the next event you attend could very well be the celebration event held in your honor to recognize your outstanding achievements as a professional event marketer. Not only will you receive the accolades you deserve, but you will continue to market this event by attracting others who wish to learn your secrets of modern event marketing success. May you use these marketing secrets to help all of us raise the level and impact of global event marketing throughout the new millennium and beyond.

Summary

In this chapter, you have learned the benefits of developing a system for ongoing competitive analysis predicated, in large part, on a comparison of the strengths, weaknesses, opportunities, and threats facing your product and those of your competitors. Comparisons of costs, timing, product differentiation, and markets being served are among the many considered, depending on the nature of the event and its present market share. Integrated efforts by management, product/program designers, and marketing professionals are critical to the development of effective monitoring of the competition and to the establishment of marketing approaches that will enhance event strengths and mitigate weaknesses. Equally important is the need to document results, not just for your event itself but also for all program participants. Evidence of the value of sponsorships, for example, is essential in maintaining and increasing those sponsorships in future years. Testimonials from pleased participants are invaluable in attracting new attendees. Underlying all of this is the careful maintenance, analysis, and archiving of all data for use in identifying competitive trends early in their life cycle and in responding effectively to those trends.

TALES FROM THE FRONT

An association with a successful East Coast exposition was interested in expanding, by adding a second trade show on the West Coast. After an extensive review of the SWOT factors, and an analysis of competitive shows on the West Coast, they discovered that they were not the first to grasp the idea. Because California is such a lucrative market in their industry, five similar corporate-sponsored shows had been launched in the same region to varying degrees of success. The competition was fierce, and the field was crowded. It just was not the time for a new little bird to pop its head out of the nest and stumble its way onto the field. The idea was not rejected. It was placed on hold for continuing competitive analysis. "Let's sit back and watch for a while" was the mantra.

Charts and grids on the competition were maintained, updated, and archived for future comparison. Close marketing intelligence was aimed at the other sponsoring corporations, as well as the performance profiles of their California expositions. Interesting trends were observed.

Seven years later, there was one show left among the original five. The continuing evaluation revealed that the market for buyers had been oversaturated, time-of-year decisions pitted too many events in too short a time span, all of the shows were in downtown areas of several major cities, and programming was repetitive. Market analysts and management saw one competitor left

and decided the time was ripe for the bird to leave the nest and set up shop in California.

They selected a mid-year month, six months removed from the remaining competitor. They analyzed sites and selected a second-tier city with excellent facilities, close to a major airport with convenient transportation systems. They offered not only fresh programming features, but also inducements such as new car giveaways and bustling bookstores of industry literature at discount prices.

The show is no longer a fledgling. After four years of careful growth designed to maintain an equitable buyer-seller ratio, the association has a solid product, a new market of attendees and members, and a waiting list for exhibit booth space. Sometimes great things do not happen overnight. But they do happen when analysts track their data religiously and then respond at the right moment.

Chapter Challenge

1. You have been asked to increase the number of your organization's event sponsors. What steps would you take to locate new sponsors, display evidence of the value of sponsorships, and leverage this growth in support to gain higher sponsorship levels among current sponsors?

2. Chart an analysis of the demographic and psychographic profiles of your market. What major value and behavioral differences would you cite between a largely World War II constituency and your emerging Generation X market segment?

Selling Summerville's Celebration to the Press

Sample Press Communications Forms and Media Releases

Following are components of a multifaceted promotional campaign for a special event in a hypothetical town in Indiana. The campaign involves print and electronic media, as well as civic leaders, sponsors, and honorees.

1. Sample Personal Letter
2. Sample News Release
3. Sample Request for Media Coverage
4. Sample Speaker's "Talking Points"
5. Sample Photo-Video Opportunity
6. Sample Video News Release (VNR)
7. Sample Audio News Release (ANR)
8. Sample Public Service Announcement (PSA)

Accolade
communications

63 N. Tascoe Drive
New Bedsfield, IN 41625
301-862-9700
FAX 301-862-1319
accolade@zypher.com

November 24, 2001

Mr. Jeffrey Baumgartner
News Editor
Summerville Daily Banner
14216 Edison Blvd.
Summerville, IN 41256

Dear Jeff:

You and I have talked about my involvement in producing the First Annual Founder's
Day Parade in Summerville, July 30, 2002, as well as the "Town Festival and Fireworks
Frenzy" that will follow that evening.

I'm delighted to say that we have assembled a terrific planning committee, led by Iona
Rogers of the Town Council. Her vision for the events to be held in our inaugural
Founder's Day festivities is extraordinary, and our plans are well enough along to make
some of the more exciting features public. While we will be holding news conferences
and issuing further information as we get closer to the dates, I thought you may be
interested in not only the events being planned but also her impressions of the positive
impact this event will have on the community for years to come.

I would deeply appreciate a call from you or the reporter to whom you assign the story, in
order to arrange an interview with Councilwoman Rogers.

Let me know which dates are most convenient for you or your reporter, and I will
coordinate those times with Mrs. Rogers. If you need more information or would like to
schedule the interview, please call me on my personal line at 301-862-9711.

Best Personal Regards,

Buck

Leonard H. Hoyle
President

63 N. Tascoe Drive
New Bedsfield, IN 41625
301-862-9700
FAX 301-862-1319
accolade@zypher.com

NEWS RELEASE

FOR IMMEDIATE RELEASE:

For More Information Call:
Barry Archibald
301-862-9716

Summerville's Founders' Day Festivities Scheduled for July 30, 2002

(Summerville, IN, Mar. 20, 2002) — The **First Annual Founders' Day Parade** will celebrate the 1892 founding of Summerville, IN, on July 30, 2002 featuring bands, floats, dignitaries and cheering crowds filling the heart of the community's downtown area. Mayor Justin Sansibald called the event a "long overdue recognition of our pride in our town, and its rich history."

The daylong series of events will be highlighted by the parade, from 2 p.m. to 4:30 p.m., followed by the Summerville **"Town Festival and Fireworks Frenzy"** at the County Fairgrounds. Food, entertainment and family fun will bring the Fairgrounds to life from 5:30 p.m. until the fireworks begin at 9 p.m. Details of the parade and festival will be announced at a press conference on April 13 by Town Councilwoman Iona Rogers, chair of the Planning Committee.

"Interest in this event is amazing," said Rogers, adding that "we expect more than 20 marching bands, at least two dozen floats, clowns, and fire engines from communities throughout the state." Admission to the parade, festival and fireworks will be free, she said.

# # #

63 N. Tascoe Drive
New Bedsfield, IN 41625
301-862-9700
FAX 301-862-1319
accolade@zypher.com

REQUEST FOR MEDIA COVERAGE

Press Conference Scheduled to Announce
Details of Summerville Founders' Day Festival

WHAT: A **Press Conference** announcing details of Summerville, Indiana's **First Annual Founders' Day Parade** and **"Town Festival and Fireworks Frenzy."** Press kits will be distributed and speakers will cover details of the events, which are expected to draw more than 15,000 attendees and numerous bands, floats, dignitaries and special marching groups. Festival arrangements for print, broadcast and electronic media coverage will be announced. A question and answer session will follow.

WHEN: April 13, 2002. Press conference begins at 10:30 a.m. with a light brunch. It is anticipated that the conference will conclude by 12 noon.

WHERE: Summerville Town Center, 1362 Broad Street, with the conference taking place in Community Hall on the first floor.

WHO: Key speakers will include Summerville Mayor Justin Sansibald, and Planning Committee Chair Iona Rogers, Town Councilwoman. Other city officials will be on hand as well, including Police Chief Rogers Laraby, Fire Chief Bruce Lichter and Director of Public Works Brenda Flemeister.

CONTACT: Barry Archibald at 301-862-9716 for any special requirements to cover the press conference. Risers will be available for television and broadcast equipment. Podium and cordless microphones will be provided. Special electrical, cable and lighting requirements should be requested by April 4, 2002.

# # #

63 No. Tascoe Drive
New Bedsfield, IN 41625
301-862-9700
FAX 301-862-1319
accolade@zypher.com

SPEAKER'S "TALKING POINTS"

TO: Councilwoman Iona Rogers

RE: These are **Key Points** to cover during your remarks at the Press
Conference on Summerville Founders' Day activities.
(Please be at Summerville Town Center no later than 10 a.m.
April 13, 2002. Conference begins at 10:30. Location will be in
Community Hall, first floor of the Center)

KEY POINTS TO COVER IN OPENING REMARKS:

- **SUMMERVILLE WILL BE 110 YEARS OLD ON JULY 30!**

- **PARADE BEGINS AT 2:00 PM, ENDS AT 4:30 PM**

- **"TOWN FESTIVAL" BEGINS 5:30 PM AT FAIRGROUNDS**

- **PARADE MARSHALLS: DORA SANDERS & THE MAYOR**

- **FREE ADMISSION. FOOD/BEVERAGES NOMINAL COST**

- **EXPECT 15,000 – 20,000 FROM AROUND THE REGION**

- **REVENUE GENERATED FOR MERCHANTS: $300,000**

- **EACH SUCCEEDING ANNUAL FESTIVAL WILL GROW**

- **PRESS CREDENTIALS WILL BE MAILED TO YOU**

- **CALL MY OFFICE FOR ANY ASSISTANCE YOU NEED**

63 N. Tascoe Drive
New Bedsfield, IN 41625
301-862-9700
FAX 301-862-1319
accolade@zypher.com

PHOTO-VIDEO OPPORTUNITY

TO: Program Directors
News Directors
Assignments Editors

WHAT: A special presentation of historical documents commemorating the founding of Summerville, IN, in 1892.

WHO: Dora Sanders, great-great granddaughter of Samuel Summer, will present Mayor Justin Sansibald with the original diary of the town's founder, describing his experiences as his inn and trading post formed the core of an infant community. Also included among the memorabilia are personal letters, illustrations, and real estate deeds and documents. Other civic leaders will be on hand for the ceremonies.

WHERE: Summerville Town Center, 1362 Broad Street. The presentations will be staged in the ground floor foyer.

WHEN: May 15, 2002 at 10 a.m. The presentations will last about 15 minutes, including short remarks. Mrs. Sanders, the Mayor and others will remain for any individual interviews requested.

WHY: The Town Council is working on a plan to archive the historical documents on display in a public area of the Summerville Town Center, in recognition of the First Annual Founders' Day Parade scheduled for July 30, 2002.

CONTACT: Barry Archibald at 301-862-9716 for further details.

63 N. Tascoe Drive
New Bedsfield, IN 41625
301-862-9700
FAX 301-862-1319
accolade@zypher.com

VIDEO NEWS RELEASE

TO: Chad Bartow, News Director, WSUM-TV

CONTACT: Barry Archibald, Press Coordinator, **Summerville Founders' Day Festivities**, 301-862-9716

DATE: June 20, 2002

On behalf of the Planning Committee for the July 30 Summerville Founders' Day Parade, Festival and Fireworks, we have prepared a video featuring interviews with Mayor Justin Sansibald and Town Councilwoman Iona Rogers, Planning Committee Chair. **The video will be hand-delivered to you on July 10, 2002.** It is designed in segments for easy editing and presentation during a series of newscasts or programs, or it can be presented in its entirety (a seamless version with segues is also provided on the videotape). Total running time: 6:10

Segment 1: (1:10) Mayor Sansibald interview in his office.

Segment 2: (1:15) Councilwoman Rogers on location at Parade sites, with graphics of Parade route and parking locations.

Segment 3: (1:35) Mayor Sansibald and Ms. Rogers on location at County Fairgrounds, with graphics of Festival and Fireworks locations.

Segment 4: (1:25) Interviews with local sponsors who are providing water stations, first aid stations, signs, banners, and food stations.

Segment 5: (:45) "Man on the Street" interviews about festivities.

63 N. Tascoe Drive
New Bedsfield, IN 41625
301-862-9700
FAX 301-862-1319
accolade@zypher.com

AUDIO NEWS RELEASE

TO: Bonnie Carter
               Dir., Local Public Affairs Programming WNOW Radio

CONTACT: Barry Archibald, Press Coordinator, **Summerville
               Founders' Day Festivities,** 301-862-9716

DATE: June 21, 2002

On behalf of the Planning Committee for the July 30
Summerville Founders' Day Parade, Festival and
Fireworks, we have prepared an audio tape featuring an
interview with Dora Sanders, great-great granddaughter
of Samuel Summer. **The audio taped interview will
be delivered to you on July 10, 2002.** Your listeners
will be fascinated by her descriptions of the memorabilia
handed down to her through the generations. She paints
a vivid portrait of the birth of Summerville through the
founder's diaries, letters, and business documents.

RUNNING TIME: (4:10)

FORMAT: May be segmented into several interviews. Mrs. Sanders
discusses the history of Summerville; reads from and cites
passages in the founder's documents; describes his
original trading post and inn and the settlers it attracted,
and talks about the importance of the commemoration to
the community and the Summer descendants.

RELEASE: At your convenience after July 10.

63 N. Tascoe Drive
New Bedsfield, IN 41625
301-862-9700
FAX 301-862-1319
accolade@zypher.com

PUBLIC SERVICE ANNOUNCEMENT

TO: Public Service Director   **CONTACT:** Barry Archibald
                                                            301-862-9716

:30 Seconds. Please run 7/15/02 through 7/30/02

DID YOU REALIZE THAT OUR TOWN OF SUMMERVILLE IS 110

YEARS OLD ON JULY 30? ON THIS SAME DATE IN 1892,

SAMUEL SUMMER ESTABLISHED HIS TRADING POST AND INN

AT THE CROSSROADS OF AMERICA'S MIDWEST, AND

SUMMERVILLE WAS BORN! WE'RE CELEBRATING THIS JULY

30 WITH THE FIRST ANNUAL "FOUNDERS' DAY PARADE"

DOWN BROAD STREET...FOLLOWED BY THE "TOWN

FESTIVAL AND FIREWORKS FRENZY" AT THE COUNTY

FAIRGROUNDS. THERE'LL BE PLENTY OF FOOD, FUN AND

FIREWORKS FOR THE WHOLE FAMILY! SEE YOU AT THE

PARADE AT 2 P.M. JULY 30TH!

APPENDIX B

Resources

Media Distribution Services

Burrelle's. Media monitoring for the digital age. **http://www.burrelles.com.**

Go Press Release. Specializes in press release writing and distribution. **http://www.gopressrelease.com.**

Internet News Bureau.com (INB). Online press release services for businesses and journalists. **http://www.newsbureau.com.**

Internet Wire. An Internet-based distributor of direct company news and other business communications materials. **http://www.internetwire.com.**

PIMS. Helps public relations professionals gain maximum benefits from their media campaigns. **http://www.pimsinc.com.**

Press-Release-Writing.com. Specializes in press release writing and press release distribution to media outlets. Also includes tips and resources for writing releases. **http://www.press-release-writing.com.**

Event Marketing Associations/Societies

American Marketing Association
311 South Wacker Drive
Suite 5800
Chicago, IL 60606
(800) AMA-1150
http://www.ama.org
A comprehensive professional society of marketers.

American Society of Association Executives
1575 I Street, NW
Washington, DC 20005
Phone: (202) 626-2723
Fax: (202) 371-0870
http://www.asaenet.org
Dedicated to enhancing the

professionalism and competency of association executives.

Association for Convention Operations Management (ACOM)
2965 Flowers Road South
Suite 105
Atlanta, GA 30341
Phone: (770) 454-9411
Fax: (770) 458-3314
http://www.acomonline.org
An international association for convention professionals.

Association of Convention Marketing Executives
1819 Peachtree Street, NE
Suite 712
Atlanta, GA 30309
(404) 355-2400
A professional trade association whose members are professional convention marketing executives.

Business Marketing Association
400 North Michigan Avenue, 15th Floor
Chicago, IL 60611
(800) 664-4BMA (4262)
http://www.marketing.org
The professional trade association that serves the professional, educational, and career development needs of business-to-business marketers.

Center for Exhibition Industry Research (CEIR)
2301 Lake Shore Drive
Suite E1002
Chicago, IL 60616
Phone: (312) 808-CEIR (2347)
Fax: (312) 949-EIPC (3472)

http://www.ceir.org
The primary research, information, and promotional arm of the exhibition industry worldwide.

Convention Industry Council (CIC)
8201 Greensboro Drive
Suite 300
McLean, VA 22102
Phone: (703) 610-9030
Fax: (703) 610-9005
http://www.c-l-c.org
Composed of leading national and international organizations involved in the meetings, conventions, expositions, and travel and tourism industries.

Exhibit Designers and Producers Association (EDPA)
5775 Peachtree-Dunwoody Road
Suite 500-G
Atlanta, GA 30342-1507
Phone: (404) 303-7310
Fax: (404) 252-0774
http://www.edpa.com
Members include exhibit designers, producers, systems manufacturers/marketers, show service contractors, exhibit transportation companies, and many other organizations that provide products or services to the exhibit industry.

Exposition Service Contractors Association (ESCA)
40 South Houston Street
Suite 210
Dallas, TX 75202
Phone: (214) 742-9217

Fax: (214) 741-2519
http://www.esca.org
The professional organization of firms engaged in the provision of materials and/or services for trade shows, conventions, exhibitions, and sales meetings.

Hospitality Sales and Marketing Association International (HSMAI)
1300 L Street, NW
Suite 800
Washington, DC 20005
(202) 789-0089
http://www.hsmai.org
A professional trade association whose members are professional salespeople in the hotel, convention center, and hospitality industry and those who provide services and products for this industry.

International Association of Conference Centers (IACC)
243 North Lindbergh Boulevard
Suite 315
St. Louis, MO 63141
Phone: (314) 993-8575
Fax: (314) 993-8919
http://www.iacconline.com
Advances the understanding and awareness of conference centers as distinct and unique within the hospitality industry.

International Association for Exhibition Management (IAEM)
5001 LBJ Freeway
Suite 350
Dallas, TX 75244
Phone: (972) 458-8002

Fax: (972) 458-8119
http://www.iaem.org
A professional association involved in the management and support of the global exposition industry.

International Communications Industries Association (ICIA)
3150 Spring Street
Fairfax, VA 22031
(703) 273-7200
The professional trade association whose members provide communications services.

International Special Events Society
9202 North Meridian Street
Suite 200
Indianapolis, IN 46260-1810
(800) 688-ISES
The only umbrella organization representing all aspects of the special events industry.

Meeting Professionals International (MPI)
4455 LBJ Freeway
Suite 1200
Dallas, TX 75244
Phone: (972) 702-3005
Fax: (972) 702-3036
http://www.mpiweb.org
Serves the diverse needs of all people with direct interest in the outcome of meetings, educating and preparing members for their changing roles and validating relevant knowledge and skills, as well as demonstrating a commitment to excellence in meetings.

National Association of Catering Executives (NACE)
5565 Sterrett Drive
Suite 328
Columbia, MD 21045
Phone: (410) 997-9055
Fax: (410) 997-8834
http://www.nace.net
A professional association for caterers in all disciplines and their affiliate vendors.

Professional Convention Management Association (PCMA)
2301 South Lake Shore Drive
Suite 1001
Chicago, IL 60616
Phone: (312) 423-7262
Fax: (312) 423-7222
http://www.pcma.org
Serves the association community by enhancing the effectiveness of meetings, conventions, and exhibitions through member and industry education and by promoting the value of the meetings industry to the general public.

Public Relations Society of America (PRSA)
33 Irvin Place
New York, NY 10003
(212) 995-2230
http://www.prsa.org
The professional trade association whose members are involved in public relations activities or supply goods and services for this profession.

Religious Conference Management Association
One RCA Dome
Suite 120
Indianapolis, IN 46225

Phone: (317) 632-1888
Fax: (317) 632-7909
Serves members planning and marketing conventions and events for religious organizations worldwide.

Society of Corporate Meeting Professionals (SCMP)
2965 Flowers Road South
Suite 105
Atlanta, GA 30341
Phone: (770) 457-9212
Fax: (770) 458-3314
http://www.scmp.org
Membership consists of corporate meeting professionals and convention/service professionals.

Trade Show Exhibitors Association (TSEA)
5501 Backlick Road
Suite 105
Springfield, VA 22151
Phone: (703) 941-3725
Fax: (703) 941-8275
http://www.tsea.org
Provides information to management professionals who utilize the trade show and event medium to promote and sell their products, as well as those who supply them with products and services.

Travel Industry Association of America (TIA)
1100 New York Avenue, NW
Washington, DC 20005
(202) 408-8422
http://www.tia.org
The professional trade association whose members promote, market, research, and provide information about the travel industry.

Media Tracking Services

Ask Network. Tracks press coverage of clients or competitors, industry, or business topics for any time period. **http://www.knowledgespace.com.**

Research on Demand. A fee-based research service, accessing public and private databases worldwide; includes media tracking services. **http://www.researchondemand.com.**

Sabela. Independent ad serving, tracking, and analysis. **http://us.www.sabela.com.**

Track Star. Offers online ad tracking and reporting services to effectively measure the success of online marketing efforts. **http://www.vitabella.com.**

TVEyes.com. Specializes in highly automated, instant-alert media tracking services for Internet users. **http://www.tveyes.com.**

Event Marketing Books

Association of National Advertisers Event Marketing Committee (1995). *Event Marketing: A Management Guide.* New York: Association of National Advertisers.

Astroff, M. T., and Abbey, J. R. (1995). *Convention Sales and Services,* 4th ed. Cranbury, NJ: Waterbury Press.

Baghot, R., and Nuttall, G. (1990). *Sponsorship, Endorsements and Merchandising: A Practical Guide.* London: Waterloo.

Bergin, R., and Hempel, E. (1990). *Sponsorship and the Arts: A Practical Guide to Corporate Sponsorship of the Performing and Visual Arts.* Evanston, IL: Entertainment Resource Group.

Catherwood, D. W., and Van Kirk, R. L. (1992). *The Complete Guide to Special Event Management: Business Insights, Financial Advice, and Successful Strategies from Ernst & Young, Advisors to the Olympics, the Emmy Awards and the PGA Tour.* New York: John Wiley & Sons.

Cohen, W. A. (1987). *Developing a Winning Marketing Plan.* New York: John Wiley & Sons.

Dance, J. (1994). *How to Get the Most Out of Sales Meetings.* Lincolnwood, IL: NTC Business Books.

Davidson, J. P., and Fay, G. A. (1991). *Selling to Giants: A Key to Become a Key Supplier to Large Corporations.* New York: McGraw-Hill.

Delacorte, T., Kimsey, J., and Halas, S. (1981). *How to Get Free Press: A Do-It-Yourself Guide to Promote Your Interests, Organizations or Business.* San Francisco: Harbor.

Flanagan, J. (1993). *Successful Fund Raising: A Complete Handbook for Volunteers and Professionals.* Chicago: Contemporary Books.

Gartell, R. B. (1994). *Destination Marketing for Convention and Visitor Bureaus,* 2nd ed. Dubuque, IA: Kendall/Hunt.

Global Media Commission Staff (1988). *Sponsorship: Its Role and Effect.* New York: International Advertising Association.

Goldblatt, J. J. (1996). *The Best Practices in Modern Event Management.* New York: John Wiley & Sons.

Goldblatt, J., and McKibben, C. (1996). *The Dictionary of Event Management.* New York: Van Nostrand-Reinhold.

Graham, S., Goldblatt, J. J., and Delpy, L. (1995). *The Ultimate Guide to Sport Event Management and Marketing.* Chicago: Irwin.

Greier, T. (1986). *Make Your Events Special: How to Produce Successful Special Events for Non-Profit Organizations.* New York: Folkworks.

Harris, T. L. (1991). *The Marketer's Guide to Public Relations: How Today's Top Companies Are Using the New PR to Gain a Competitive Edge.* New York: John Wiley & Sons.

International Association of Business Communicators (1990). *Special Events Marketing.* San Francisco: International Association of Business Communicators.

International Events Group (1995). *Evaluation: How to Help Sponsors Measure Return on Investment.* Chicago: International Events Group.

International Events Group (1995). *Media Sponsorship: Structuring Deals with Newspaper, Magazine, Radio and TV Sponsors.* Chicago: International Events Group.

Jeweler, S., and Goldblatt, J. (2000). *The Event Management Certificate Program Event Sponsorship.* Washington, DC: George Washington University.

Kawasaki, G. (1991). *Selling the Dream: How to Promote Your Product, Company or Ideas—and Make a Difference—Using Everyday Evangelism.* New York: Harper Collins.

Keegan, P. B. (1990). *Fundraising for Non-Profits.* New York: Harper Perennial.

Kurdle, A. E., and Sandler, M. (1995). *Public Relations for Hospitality Managers.* New York: John Wiley & Sons.

Martin, E. L. (1992). *Festival Sponsorship Legal Issues.* Port Angeles, WA: International Festivals Association.

National Association of Broadcasters (1991). *A Broadcaster's Guide to Special Events and Sponsorship Risk Management.* Washington, DC: National Association of Broadcasters.

Plessner, G. M. (1980). *The Encyclopedia of Fund Raising: Testimonial Dinner and Luncheon Management Manual.* Arcadia, CA: Fund Raisers, Inc.

Quain, B. (1993). *Selling Your Services to the Meetings Market.* Dallas: Meeting Professionals International.

Reed, M. H. (1989). *IEG Legal Guide to Sponsorship.* Chicago: International Events Group.

Schmader, S. W., and Jackson, R. (1990). *Special Events: Inside and Out: A "How-to" Approach to Event Production, Marketing, and Sponsorship.* Champaign, IL: Sagamore Publishing.

Schreibner, A. L., and Lenson, B. (1994). *Lifestyle and Event Marketing: Building the New Customer Partnership.* New York: McGraw-Hill.

Shaw, M. (1990). *Convention Sales: A Book of Readings.* East Lansing, MI: Educational Institute of the American Hotel & Motel Association.

Sheerin, M. (1984). *How to Raise Top Dollars for Special Events.* Hartsdale, NY: Public Service Materials Center.

Shenson, H. L. (1990). *How to Develop and Promote Successful Seminars and Workshops: A Definitive Guide to Creating and Marketing Seminars, Classes and Conferences.* New York: John Wiley & Sons.

Simerly, R. (1990). *Planning and Marketing Conferences and Workshops: Tips, Tools, and Techniques.* San Francisco: Jossey-Bass.

Simerly, R. G. (1993). *Strategic Financial Management for Conferences, Workshops, and Meetings.* San Francisco: Jossey-Bass.

Soares, E. J. (1991). *Promotional Feats: The Role of Planned Events in the Marketing Communications Mix.* New York: Quirum Books.

Ukman, L. (1999). *IEG's Complete Guide to Sponsorship.* Chicago: International Events Group.

Waldorf, J., and Rutherford-Silvers, J. (2000). *The Event Management Certificate Program Sport Event Management and Marketing.* Washington, DC: George Washington University.

Wilkinson, D. *A Guide to Effective Event Management and Marketing.* Willowdale, Ontario: Event Management and Marketing Institute.

Williams, W. (1994). *User Friendly Fundraising: A Step-by-Step Guide to Profitable Special Events.* Alexander, NC: WorldComm.

Wolf, T. (1983). *Presenting Performances: A Handbook for Sponsors.* New York: American Council of the Arts.

Wolfson, S. M. (1995). *The Meeting Planner's Complete Guide to Negotiating: You Can Get What You Want.* Kansas City, MO: Institute for Meeting and Conference Management.

Event Marketing Periodicals

Advertising Age. Weekly, by Bill Publications, Chicago.

Agenda New York. Annually, by Agenda USA, Inc., 686 Third Avenue, New York, NY 10017; (800) 523-1233.

Association Meetings. Bimonthly, by Adams/Laux Publishing Company, 63 Great Road, Maynard, MA 01754; (508) 897-5552.

Conference and Association World. Bimonthly, by ACE International,

Riverside House, High Street, Huntingdon, Cambridgeshire PE18 6SG, England; (0480) 457595; international, 011 44 1480 457595.

Conference and Expositions International. Monthly, by International Trade Publications Ltd., Queensway House, 2 Queensway, Redhill, Surrey RH1 1QS, England; (0737) 768611; international, 011 44 1737 768611.

Conference & Incentive Management. Bimonthly, by CIM Verlag für Conference, Incentive & Travel Management GmBH, Nordkanalstrasse 36, D-20097 Hamburg, Germany; international, 40 237 1405.

Convene. Ten times a year, by Professional Convention Management Association, 100 Vestavia Office Park, Suite 220, Birmingham, AL 35216-9970; (205) 978-4911.

Conventions and Expositions. Bimonthly, by Conventions and Expositions Section of the American Society of Association Executives, 1575 I Street, NW, Washington, DC 20005; (202) 626-2769.

Corporate and Incentive Travel. Monthly, by Coastal Communications Corporation, 488 Madison Avenue, New York, NY 10022; (212) 888-1500.

Corporate Meetings and Incentives. Bimonthly, by the Laux Company, 63 Great Road, Maynard, MA 01754; (508) 897-5552.

Corporate Travel. Monthly, by Miller Freeman, Inc., 1515 Broadway, New York, NY 10036; (212) 626-2501.

Delegates. Monthly, by Audrey Brindsley, Premier House, 10 Greycoat Place, London SW1P 1SB, England; (0712) 228866.

Entertainment Marketing Letter. Twelve times a year, by EPM Communications, Inc., 488 East 18th Street, Brooklyn, NY 11226-6702; (718) 469-9330.

Events. Bimonthly, by April Harris, published by Harris Communications, Madison, AL.

Events Magazine. Monthly, 1080 North Delaware Street, Suite 1700, Philadelphia, PA 19125; (215) 426-7800.

Event Solutions. Monthly, by Virgo Publishing, Inc., Phoenix, AZ; (602) 990-1101.

Events USA. Suite 301, 386 Park Avenue South, New York, NY 10016; (212) 684-2222.

Event World. Monthly by International Special Events Society, Indianapolis, IN.

Festival Management & Event Tourism. Quarterly, by Cognizant Communication Corp., 3 Hartsdale Road, Elmsford, NY 10523-3701.

Incentive. Monthly, by Bill Communications, Inc., 770 Broadway, New York, NY 10003; (646) 654-4500.

M&C Meetings and Conventions. By News American Publishing, Inc., 747 Third Avenue, New York, NY 10017.

Marketing Review. By Hospitality Sales and Marketing Association International, 1400 K Street, NW, Suite 810, Washington, DC 20005.

The Meeting Manager. By Meeting Professionals International, 1950 Stemmons Freeway, Dallas, TX 75207.

Meeting News. By Gralla Publications, 1515 Broadway, New York, NY 10036.

Public Relations Journal. 845 Third Avenue, New York, NY 10022.

Religious Conference Manager Magazine, published seven times a year by PRIMEDIA, 175 Nature Valley Place, Owatonna, MN 55060 507-455-2136.

Sales and Marketing Management. Fifteen times a year, by Bill Communications, Inc., 770 Broadway, New York, NY 10003; (646) 654-4500.

Special Events Forum. Six times annually, by Dave Nelson, 1973 Schrader Drive, San Jose, CA 95124.

Special Events Magazine. Monthly, by PRIMEDIA, 1440 Broadway, New York, NY 10018.

Successful Meetings. Thirteen times a year, by Goldstein and Associates, Inc., 1150 Yale Street, #12, Santa Monica, CA 90403; (310) 828-1309.

Tradeshow Week. Weekly, by Tradeshow Week, 12233 West Olympic Boulevard, #236, Los Angeles, CA 90064; (310) 826-5696.

Electronic Marketing Services

Aelana Interactive Multimedia Development. http://www.aelana.com.

Aspen Media. Creative solutions for the digital age. http://www.aspenmedia.com.

Bay Area Marketing. Specializes in Web design, site promotion, hosting, and more. http://www.bayareamarketing.com.

d2m Interactive. A full-service Web development company that offers custom Web site design, Web presence management, Internet marketing services, and electronic commerce solutions. http://www.d2m.com/index2.html.

Desktop Innovations. http://www.desktopinnovations.com.

Digital Rose. Specializes in Web site design, Internet publications, and digital photography and marketing. http://www.digital-rose.com.

Electronic Marketing Group. http://www.empg.com.

Imirage, E-business. Technology and interactive marketing solutions. http://www.imirage.com.

Impact Studio. Uses the Internet, CD-ROM, and digital video to create electronic marketing campaigns. http://www.impactstudio.com.

Information Strategies. Electronic marketing, consulting, information design, Web assistance, organizational development for information technology issues. **http://www.info-strategies.com.**

Ironwood Electronic Media. Offers electronic marketing services for businesses. **http://www.cris.com/~ironwood/iwbusiness.htm.**

Magic Hour Communications. http://www.magic-hour.com.

SpectraCom. Provides strategic planning and electronic marketing services. **http://www.spectracom.com.**

Facility/Venue Directories

America's Meeting Places. Published by Facts on File.

Auditorium/Arena/Stadium Guide. Published by Amusement Business/Single Copy Department, Box 24970, Nashville, TN 37202.

International Association of Conference Centers Directory. Published by International Association of Conference Centers, 45 Progress Parkway, Maryland Heights, MO 63043.

Locations, etc: The Directory of Locations and Services for Special Events. Published by Innovative Productions.

The Guide to Campus and Non-Profit Meeting Facilities. Published by AMARC.

Tradeshow and Convention Guide. Published by Amusement Business/Single Copy Department, Box 24970, Nashville, TN 37202.

References

Ashman, S. G., and Ashman, J. (1999). *Introduction to Event Information Systems.* Washington, DC: George Washington University.

Catalano, F., and Smith, B. (2001). *Internet Marketing for Dummies.* Foster City, CA: IDG Books Worldwide.

Catherwood, D. W., and Van Kirk, R. L. (1992). *The Complete Guide to Special Event Management, Business Insights, Financial Advice, and Successful Strategies from Ernst & Young, Advisors to the Olympics, the Emmy Awards and the PGA Tour.* New York: John Wiley & Sons.

Cohen, W. A. (1987). *Developing a Winning Marketing Plan.* New York: John Wiley & Sons.

Diamond, C. (2000). "Marketing/Reg. Tool Is Hailed as Next Big Thing." *Meeting News,* November 6.

Dolan, K., Kerrins, D., and Kasofsky, G. (2000). *Internet Event Marketing.* Washington, DC: George Washington University.

Eager, B., and McCall, C. (1999). *The Complete Idiot's Guide to Online Marketing.* QUE.

Fried, K., Goldblatt, J., and Rutherford-Silvers, J. (2000). *Event Marketing.* Washington, DC: George Washington University.

Goldblatt, J. (2001). *Special Events, Twenty-First Century Global Event Management.* New York: John Wiley & Sons, Inc.

Keeler, L. (1995). *Cyber Marketing.* AMACOM.

Jeweler, S., and Goldblatt, J. (2000). *The Event Management Certificate Program Event Sponsorship.* Washington, DC: George Washington University.

Judson, B. (1996). *Net Marketing—Your Guide to Profit and Success on the Net.* Wolff New Media.

Lang, E. (2001). "Six Essential E-Mails for Registrants." *Association Meetings,* June.

Mack, T. (2000). "Electronic Marketing: What You Can Expect." *The Futurist,* March/April.

Rich, J. R. (2001). *The Unofficial Guide to Marketing Your Business Online.* Foster City, CA: IDG Books Worldwide.

Rosa, J. (1999). "E-commercials: Revolutionizing Electronic Marketing." *Computer Reseller News,* August 23.

Sterne, J. (2001). *World Wide Web Marketing: Integrating the Web Into Your Marketing Strategy.* New York: John Wiley & Sons.

Ukman, L. (1999). *IEG's Complete Guide to Sponsorship.* Chicago: International Events Group.

US Web, and Bruner, R. E. (1998). *Net Results: Web Marketing That Works.* New Riders.

Waldorf, J., and Rutherford-Silvers, J. (2000). *The Event Management Certificate Program Sport Event Management and Marketing.* Washington, DC: George Washington University.

Whitman, D. "Exchange Links and Lure New Customers—for Free." *Net Progress.* Microsoft Central.com.

Index